A BRIEF DISPLAY OF
THE ORIGIN AND HISTORY OF ORDEALS;

TRIALS BY BATTLE; COURTS OF CHIVALRY OR HONOUR;

AND THE

DECISION OF PRIVATE QUARRELS BY SINGLE COMBAT:

ALSO,

A CHRONOLOGICAL REGISTER

OF

THE PRINCIPAL DUELS

FOUGHT FROM THE ACCESSION OF HIS LATE MAJESTY
TO THE PRESENT TIME.

BY JAMES P. GILCHRIST

The Naval & Military Press Ltd

published in association with

ROYAL ARMOURIES

Published by
The Naval & Military Press Ltd
Unit 10 Ridgewood Industrial Park,
Uckfield, East Sussex,
TN22 5QE England
Tel: +44 (0) 1825 749494
Fax: +44 (0) 1825 765701
www.naval-military-press.com

in association with

ROYAL ARMOURIES

In reprinting in facsimile from the original, any imperfections are inevitably reproduced and the quality may fall short of modern type and cartographic standards.

TO

FIELD MARSHAL, HIS ROYAL HIGHNESS

PRINCE FREDERICK,

DUKE OF YORK,

K. G. AND G. C. B.,
&c. &c. &c.

Sir,

The honour which your Royal Highness has done me in condescending to peruse this work, previously to its publication, I shall ever feel as the most flattering mark of approbation which it can possibly receive. And the sentiments which your Royal Highness has expressed to me concerning it, have altogether deprived me of those feelings which another person in my situation would experience, and robbed me of that utterance which should grace my Dedication.

DEDICATION.

Yet with submission and delicacy, I shall endeavour to express how much I am honoured by the condescension of your Royal Highness, in devoting the few hours of relaxation which your numerous duties yielded you, to read my Treatise, in all its parts; and in deeming it of importance enough to appear before the British Nation, bearing this unequivocal mark of your Royal Highness's illustrious patronage.

Your Royal Highness, who is acquainted with the circumstances which gave rise to the compilation of this work, could enter with feelings becoming a Prince and a judge, into all the various portions of historical and biographical narrative, of which it is composed, and decide upon their utility and truth, without prejudice in favour of an usage that distinguished itself chiefly in the profession, over which your Royal Highness presides; and without any misconception as to the motives which have induced me to appear before the Army, and the people of Great Britain, as an Author, honoured

DEDICATION.

with the gracious and powerful protection of your Royal Highness.

Next to the approbation of His Most Gracious Majesty, is the distinguished sanction of the Commander in Chief and Heir Presumptive; and proud indeed am I to enjoy the felicity of this high honour. Another person more gifted than myself would seize the occasion to expatiate on the character of your Royal Highness; but as it is the privilege of a dedicator to praise his Patron without offence, I may be permitted to say, that in the person of your Royal Highness are concentrated the courage of a soldier, and the prudence of a general, the dignity of a prince, and the humanity of a patriot. I but speak a truth, known to all the world, when I advert to the unremitting assiduity with which the entire powers of your Royal Highness's enlightened and liberal understanding, have been devoted to the comfort, and the happiness of every officer and private soldier, under the command of your Royal Highness:

and I furnish no intelligence to mankind, when I bring before them, the impartiality and benevolence of your Royal Highness's humane disposition, in redressing the wrongs of the aggrieved, in righting the injuries of the oppressed, should such be the misfortune of any humble individual, over whom the power of your Royal Highness extends; and in gaining the unshaken confidence and unbiassed affection of all those, who have the happiness to be placed under your Royal Highness's more immediate authority. I should raise my voice in vain, were I to dilate on those virtues, which have characterized the life of your Royal Highness.

It is my business, Sir, rather to admire than applaud them; they receive the tribute of a nation's gratitude, whenever, and wherever, your Royal Highness appears. And I must be content in being one of the very many, who pay to those virtues the silent homage of the heart; for the best things that I might say, could not render your Royal Highness dearer to Britons; and that I may not suffer in the good opinion of your Royal Highness, by overstepping the limits which my duty prescribes, I will rather become a loser in the judgement of the Public, for having said so little.

I have the honour to be,

Sir,

Your Royal Highness's

Most devoted, faithful, and

Obedient Humble Servant,

JAMES P. GILCHRIST.

London,
October 1, 1821.

PREFACE.

In arranging for my own satisfaction and amusement the materials of this work, which I have the honour of laying before the British Public, I formed those conceptions of the usage in question—of its nature—of its operation—and its results—which are interspersed in various parts of these pages; and in pursuance of this plan, I have gone through a long, but interesting train of reading and examination, with the sole view of giving to my mind a *fair* and *impartial picture* of the subject, without those extraneous accompaniments which are peculiar to legal compositions; and in this shape, in which I placed it before my unlearned mind, I now present it, stript of legal dress, and appearing under that figure, which, I hope, may ensure facility of comprehension, and consequent instruction. My brief display pretends to no learning—no recondite research, or profound argumentation. It merely offers that view of an interesting part of British Law, and ancient usage, which an individual would wish to take, without being subject to the trammels of Legal Phraseology, or the labour of study. I was desirous of tracing the degree of resemblance in those numerous and celebrated personal combats, of which I had previously heard so much. My researches becoming extensive, and the matter voluminous, I was ultimately induced to make a systematic arrangement of those combats, the accounts of which appeared sufficiently authentic and appropriate to my purpose.

Conceiving that a collection which, in this accidental way, had amused and interested myself, might prove a source of interest and amusement to others, and particularly to the Military part of the British Public, I have attached it to the other subjects of this work, as highly illustrative of the strides, which the iniquitous practice of duelling has made, towards establishing itself in the bosom of civilized Society. I am aware of the possibility, and even probability, of error, and would have been happy, had I been able to adduce in favour of *all*, the same undoubted proofs of authenticity, which attach to the great majority of cases; and, particularly, if I could have given a clear narrative of some interesting contests, which are known to many individuals, but of which no account has been made public. It will be observed, upon a very superficial glance at the contents of this Volume, that its details are chiefly confined to the operation of the practice in question, upon two distinct classes of gentlemen,—the Officers of the Army and Navy—I may therefore be allowed to offer a few remarks upon their profession, and the hardships to which they are exposed, when called upon by a deliberate challenge, to transgress the awful laws of God and their Country: for it will be admitted upon all sides, a high tone of honourable feeling has ever been assumed, and with persevering consistency maintained by the British Army: thence an imperative duty arises, which calls upon every individual, connected with that renowned body, to justify this assumption and this character, in his own personal capacity.

It is also reasonable to suppose, that a vivid feeling of this description is indulged by every young man, when he forms the deliberate resolution of devoting himself to military pursuits; and that the importance of his station, on his becoming a British Officer, has a powerful tendency to invigorate and mature those just principles, which are the usual accompaniments of a respectable rank in life, and of a liberal education.

But it is nevertheless possible, that the fervour of the youthful character may, in some instances, overstep the bound of rational controul; that a judgment, not yet ripened by experience, may draw unfortunate conclusions; and that evils may, thus, result, which may ultimately become the copious subjects of painful and lasting regret.

Yet these instances are rare: for ample are the means of acquiring correct conceptions of that mutual urbanity which forms the bond, and the security of social communication in the Army, and which acts as a powerful preventative against those evils which, otherwise, might too frequently occur.

Unfortunate occasions of this description, however, do sometimes arise, involving consequences acutely painful to the principal actors, in their individual capacity, and offering ample materials of reflection to two classes of persons: —to Officers of the Army, in the first instance, and to the enlightened friends of society, in the second.

PREFACE. xiii

I do not presume to be casuist sufficient to enter into all the moral niceties, connected with the subject of Single Combats. I am not prepared, nor is it necessary to the full comprehension of those difficulties with which the duty of every man and every soldier, is fraught, to come to a decision on the best grounds of reconciling the criminal law of a great nation with the laws of honour; or, the appropriate means of disarming the penal terrors of the one, when the utmost claims of the other are perfectly satisfied. It may also be unnecessary, to retrace the origin of this mode of redressing private wrongs to those barbarous times when the interference of Heaven was confidently expected to aid the arm of the man who, with the advantage of right in his quarrel, appealed to the decision of his sword; or, when the continent virgin, fearlessly submitted to the "burning share" as a certain test of chastity. I am willing to admit that present usages are to be preferred in the exact proportion, in which they purge the Institutes of a great people from such impure mixture of Law and Superstitious Custom, and place all matter of public and private wrong, and public and private redress, on the unerring basis of Reason and Justice: for no man can bend with more implicit reverence to the Institutions of his Country on this ground, than the compiler of this work.

It may however be necessary to state the possibility of establishing, in the bosom of the Army, a Court of Honour, vested with ample authority for the investigation of all personal disputes, and armed with adequate power for the due punishment of every deviation from that line of honourable deportment, which is so peculiarly necessary among military associates. But this is an extended field of moral and judicial argument, upon which my profession, and the peculiar line of my reflections, do not warrant a decided opinion. I may, however, be permitted to speak with more decision, respecting the present usage of the British Army, and the actual and possible evils, to which a British Officer may be exposed, even when observing the principles of the nicest discretion, in every part of his temper and deportment. Such an individual, it imports not on what subject, receives an insult from a Brother Officer, or any Gentleman. He justly demands a reasonable apology for an unmerited offence—the apology is refused, and possibly under circumstances of additional insult, or aggravation.

PREFACE.

If at this moment he hesitates—if he allows his preconceived notions of morality and religion to " weigh a feather" in the scale of his determination, he is *lost for ever* as a *British Officer.* It matters not, if before that momentous hour, he had supported a character for more than mortal bravery—if he had mounted the *" deadly breach"* in his *" Country's cause,"* or faced the *" Cannon's mouth." No plea* is granted for a moment's hesitation.—The devoted victim to a MISTAKEN principle, *must* send the fatal message,* or endure a consequent suffering, worse than death to an honourable mind—the destruction of his fame and fortune as a military man.

But let us pursue the challenge under the most legitimate circumstances of an unfortunate result. Let us grant that, previous to the message which he is compelled to send, his conduct has been most correct, that, that correctness is preserved with the most scrupulous nicety by himself and his friend on the fatal field, that

---

* The result is here fraught with singular uncertainty; the consequences having sometimes proved as full of hazard to the seconds as to the principals; when experience has demonstrated, that he who fell was fortunate to escape the ignominy of a judicial sentence, consigning the survivors to death or irretrievable loss of character.

neither of them subsequently shrink from the cognizance of the criminal law of their country —that the Coroner's Jury, in due form, charges them and their accessories with the crime of murder—that the Grand Inquest of the country, on the presentment of the bill of indictment, find it true ;—and finally, that they are placed *at the Bar* of their *offended Country*.—This is the terrific cup of sorrow, which a barbarous and relentless usage has presented to many; the cup out of which they have been compelled to drink to the very lees ;—for this great nation allows no competitor in her administration of justice, even in personal wrongs ;—she allows not even to her brave and honourable defenders, the right of redressing their own injuries, in a way of their own choosing ; nor will she suffer individuals to withdraw from under her sacred sceptre, and avenge themselves in the punishment of the insolent, or the chastisement of the haughty and the uncontrolled.* I trust that

* No man can be criminal without a criminal intention: God alone can look into the heart, and man, could he look into it, has no jurisdiction over it, until society is disturbed by its actions ;—the criminal mind being the source of all criminality, the law seeks only to punish actions which it can trace to evil disposition—it pities our errors and mistakes, makes allowances for our passions, and scourges only our crimes.

I see, in its true light, the Spirit of the National Laws; but my discernment enables me not to draw the line, though I know it is attempted in such cases. For I am persuaded, that, in the *exact degree,* in which the general jurisprudence of this country is founded in *right principles,* the *present usage* of the Army is founded in those of an *opposite nature.* And hence, that unsettled contrariety between Civil Law, and Military Honour, which occasionally elicits cases of extraordinary evil to the parties immediately concerned, and of the nicest delicacy to those exalted personages, who are ultimately called upon to decide by their interfering views. Appalling is the evil if a British Officer receives an insult, and do not instantly take that notice of it which military usage requires: and equally appalling is the evil if he do; and thus pursue it to a fatal issue. I am aware, that under the present constitution of the Army, no fair combatants will ever suffer the final and ignominious penalty of the law. That Royal clemency* will, in all cases, which are fairly represented,

---

* The case of Major Campbell was not of this description. The particulars of evidence, stated in a more advanced part of this work, leave an indelible impression of unfair conduct, and consequent just execution.

interfere and snatch from an ignominious fate men of honourable minds—men to whom no " malice prepense" can, for a moment, be ascribed; or against whom no unfair proceedings can be substantiated. But why should they be placed in the possible line of undergoing such a horrific test of their understandings and their feelings?

In this age of legislative investigation,* when every usage, every principle, affecting large portions of the community—or, its whole mass, have become the subject of examination in committees of our enlightened legislators, would it be beneath their paternal care, to consider the situation of the honourable defenders of their country in this momentous respect, and educe such a system, from their investigation, as to fix, on their best basis, the honour, the urbanity, and the social intercourse of military men? Under particular circumstances, a British Officer has at present only the option between infamy, on the one hand, and the infraction of the Articles of War, in combination with the whole mass of *civil, moral,* and *religious injunctions,*

* See Legislative enquiries into the important subjects of Education—the conduct of public Charities—Police—Mendicity—Pauperism, &c. &c.

on the other. And can it be the subject of a moment's surprise, that the latter must, and ever will be, the choice of every man, and *especially* of every young man, who makes the profession of arms the object of his fond election : and feels the conviction, that a stain on his courage is paramount to every possible consideration ?—It matters not what moralists may say on this subject, or jurists advance; every military man knows, and no one knows it better than the illustrious Prince, who is at the head of the Army, that, as things now are, every Officer of honourable feelings, is compelled, under the circumstances already stated, to act in the way already described.

If these remarks are the result of an unbiassed examination into the operation and bearing of this remorseless usage, as it affects British Officers, and that it is, I do affirm, without fear of contradiction; is it not matter of surprise, that its baneful influence has not ere this become the subject of investigation in that quarter, which alone could give adequate force to restraining laws that would at once crush this malignant pestilence of Society : an evil of its magnitude and destructive operation has only, I apprehend, to be presented in its native guise, stript of those decorative palliatives which give it currency, to be looked upon by mankind with abhorrence and disgust. Should this matter become the subject of investigation by more enlightened and diversified talent, and thus be disseminated into the bosom of Society with interesting effect, happy indeed shall I be to contemplate the pleasure, that my humble exertions have, in a minor degree, stimulated the benevolent and the good, to place in its true light, this emanation of barbarous law, and superstitious custom. The consideration of this subject has engaged the attention of some of the ablest politicians of Europe; and it may not be irrelevant to quote a few of their opinions: at the head of these I would place the Duc de Sully, a man whose courage was only surpassed by his justice, whose honesty and patriotism raised France from bankruptcy to wealth, from anarchy to tranquillity: he says, "I shall conclude the memoirs of the present year, with an article, which I am already certain will have the approbation of all just and sensible persons; and for which I am also as secure of their acknowledgements. In all the principal cities of the kingdom, especially those which have arsenals and academies, there are also schools for the young nobility, in which are all kinds of sports and exercises, as well military, as those designed merely to form a graceful carriage, and give strength and activity to the limbs; and these exercises are no where more carefully cultivated than at Paris, where the spacious courts of the Arsenal, destined to this use, are full almost every hour in the day. I was always of the same opinion as Henry concerning these exercises: he often asserted, that they were the most solid foundation, not only of discipline and other military virtues, but also of those nobler sentiments, and that elevation of mind which give one nation the preeminence over every other. I used to be present at them myself, when I could steal a moment from business, as well through the taste I had for such amusements; as because I thought my presence would excite a laudable emulation amongst the youth.

"One afternoon, in carnival time, when these sports were most frequent, I left my closet to shew myself to this assembly of young men, and came very seasonably to prevent the consequences of two quarrels, which, from that mistaken notion of honour to which France has made herself a slave, were likely to have been very fatal. These quarrels had taken their rise from a trifle, as it generally happens with the greatest part of those which have been followed by the most bloody catastrophes; but the King (I am grieved to say it) took so little care to enforce the observation of the edicts published by some of his predecessors, against that barbarous custom of duelling, that every day, and for the slightest occasions, some blood was shed. I thought it my duty to endeavour to convince these young men who crowded about me, of the error they were in with regard to true valour; It is, said I to them, in fields of war, and in actions which have the service of our country in view, that courage is permitted to be shown; that which arms us against our friends, or countrymen, in contempt of all laws, as well divine as human, is but a brutal fierceness, madness, and real pusillanimity." I perceived, that the moral I endeavoured to inculcate appeared very strange to these young men, who were carried away by the heat of blood and ardour of youth: one of them, who, it was apparent, sought to give himself consequence with his fellows, replied, that Princes having at all times permitted, nay authorised duels, they had passed into custom, which holds the place of a law.

"I contented myself for the present with making the youth sensible that he supported his argument upon false and erroneous principles, and with preventing the challenge from proceeding any further; but as soon as I retired, I gave free course to my reflections upon the singularity of an abuse, unknown to the most polished, and at the same time bravest people. These reflections, when thrown upon paper, composed a kind of memorial, which I thought it my duty to present to the King.

"Duels, it is true, are of long standing in France, and indeed in Europe, but in that part only that has been overwhelmed by barbarians, from whose time this hateful custom takes its date, and appears therefore to be derived from them; and if histories of times more remote, such as that of the Emperor Otho the first, and that of the divorce of Lotharia, give some instances of single combat, they may be opposed by prohibition of equal antiquity issued out by the power of the church, as that of the Council of Valentia in 855, or by temporal authority.

"We have in France a very ancient edict, which forbids them in all civil causes, and in criminal causes limits them to five cases; high-treason, rape, house-burning, murder, and nightly theft. Saint Lewis afterwards took away all restriction; and when Philip the IVth, his grandson, seemed to restore them, 1303, in charges of State crimes, rapes, and house-burning, to which he reduced them, he was incited only by a motive at once deserving praise and censure; the hope of abolishing insensibly this custom of bloodshed, which had gathered strength in his time, by confining it to these rare cases set down in a positive law: to make this more evident, he forbad all manner of persons to allow them, by receiving what was called pledges of battle, and declared that right reserved to himself alone.

"To shew, by explaining the difference between the ancient duels, and those of our time, what a number of nameless abuses have crept into practice, which itself was from its first original corruption, it will be sufficient to lay down the circumstances and formalities which were observed in those times.

"In the first place, nobody, however offended, might take vengeance in his own right; and as it is now practised in the first emotion of caprice and passion, and much less in mere bravado, which in my opinion, is of all things the most contrary to the laws of society. They had their judges, before whom he that thought himself injured in his honour, was to give an account of the wrong suffered, and demand permission to prove, in the way of arms, that he did not lay upon his enemy a false accusation. It was then considered as shameful to desire blood for blood. The judge, who was commonly the lord of the place, made the person accused, appear before him; and never allowed the decision of battle, which was demanded by throwing a glove, or some other pledge upon the ground, but when he could get no other proof either of guilt or innocence.

"The pledges were received, and the judge deferred the decision of the quarrel to the end of two months, during the first of which the two enemies were delivered each of them to common friends, upon security for their forthcoming: their friends endeavoured by all sorts of means to discover the person criminal, and to give him a sense of the injustice of maintaining a falsehood; from which he could expect nothing but the loss of reputation, of his life, and of his soul; for they were persuaded, with the utmost degree of certainty, that heaven always gave the victory to the right cause; and therefore a duel, in their opinion, was an action of which the event could be determined by no human power.

"When the two months were expired the two rivals were put into a close prison, and committed to the ecclesiastics, who employed every motive to make them change their design. If, after all this, they still persisted, a day was at last fixed to end their quarrel.

"When the day was come, the two champions were brought fasting in the morning before the same judge, who obliged both of them to declare upon oath that they said the truth, after which they suffered them to eat; they were then armed in his presence, the kind of arms being likewise settled: four seconds, chosen with the same ceremonies, saw them undressed, and anointed all over the body with oil, and saw their beards and hair cut close. They were then conducted into an inclosed ground, and guarded by armed men, having been made to repeat, for the last time, their assertions and accusations. They were not even then suffered to advance to the combat; that moment their seconds joined them at the two ends of the field for another ceremony, which of itself was enough to make their weapons drop from their hands, at least if there had been any friendship between them. Their seconds made them join hands, with the fingers of one put between the fingers of the other; they demanded justice from one another, and were conjured on each side not to support a falsity; they solemnly promised to act upon terms of honour, and not to aim at the victory by fraud and inchantment.

"The seconds examined their arms piece by piece, to see that nothing was wanting, and then conducted them to the two ends of the lists, where they made them say their prayers and make their confession; then asking each of them whether he had any message to send to his adversary, they suffered them to advance, which they did at the signal of the herald, who cried from without the lists, "Let the brave combatants go."

"After this, it is true, they fought without mercy, and the vanquished, dead or alive, incurred all the infamy of the crime and the punishment; he was dragged upon a hurdle in his shirt, and afterwards hanged or burnt, while the other returned honoured and triumphant, with a decree that attested him to have gained his suit, and allotted him all manner of satisfaction.

"There is throughout all this ceremony something wild and ridiculous; but, however, the voice of reason, authority, and prudence, is still heard, though its dictates are utterly mistaken; whereas there is nothing but monstrous unreasonableness in the practice of those smart youths, who withdraw slily into a field to shed the blood of one another, with hands impelled by no better instinct than that which instigates a beast of prey. If men went to fight with the same coolness and deliberation as in former times, can it be imagined that there would be the hundredth part of the duels that now happen? But men have thought it necessary to dismiss consideration from that action, which is serious above all others: some rush blindly into this danger, others please themselves with being born for the destruction of their fellow creatures; others revive the hateful trade of the gladiators, and are indeed more dreadful and contemptible than the men that bore that name were heretofore.

"The forms of duels which were observed in Germany, differ not essentially from those of France which I have described: they were likewise received in Spain and England; only he who yielded to his adversary upon a single word was reputed infamous; he could not afterwards either cut his beard, bear any office, wear a weapon, or mount a horse. On the contrary, he who died in a courageous defence was buried honourably. Another singularity, which must have kept duels from being common in Germany, was, that there were *only three places* where they could be fought, Witzbourgh in Franconia, Uspach, and Hall in Swabia.

" I could not wait for His Majesty's return to Paris, to communicate to him the memorial of which I have now mentioned the contents; to inform him of the accidents to which this practice gave occasion; and to desire him to put a stop to an evil which was every day spreading by his indulgence. I entreated him to attend to the counsel which I had presumed to give him, to renew the edicts against duels, to aggravate the punishment considerably, and execute it severely, and to forbid all men to prosecute any word of injury or offence otherwise than by course of law; but to manage so, that the justice obtained might be speedy and satisfactory; to make the complainant easy, and the aggressor penitent; and lastly, to have this new order fixed up, at the beginning of every year, in the courts of the Louvre, the palace, the

Arsenal, and in other places that were most frequented. It is certain, as I represented to His Majesty, that a reputation for personal valour, *such as the Prince had established,* was able to give an edict concerning duels twice the authority that it could derive from mere royal pleasure; but the pleasure of the master of kings, a power far superior, did not allow to the reign of Henry the Great, the extirpation of this abuse. His Majesty, however, caused an extraordinary council to assemble at Fontainbleau, being resolved to examine into this matter thoroughly, and desired to know, the origin of the different forms, and customs, used in duelling. His counsellors gave him no cause to compliment them upon their erudition: all remained silent, and myself as well as others; but with such expression in my looks, as made the King easily perceive that I only wanted his command to speak. His Majesty then turned towards me, and said, " Grand Master, by your looks, I guess you know more than you pretend to know: I entreat; nay, I command you to tell us your thoughts." I made a speech, and declared my sentiments without reserve, and the Edict* for the prevention of duels which fol-

* This edict was promulgated in 1609. It obliges those

lowed I took care to send immediately into my government, and to have it observed there with the utmost strictness."

Various are the methods that have been in use in states governed by law, and in those under despotic dominion, for the suppression of duelling: we find in the Code of Christophe, the late sovereign of Hayti, a method which is at once concise and effectual, and though the adoption of it might not suit the genuine feelings of Englishmen, but be a blot on our highly enlightened system of jurisprudence, it is, notwithstanding, a further elucidation, that the evil is not without a remedy.

"The King," says the Code Henri, "particularly forbids, under any pretence whatever, the officers of the army, and other individuals belonging to it, to make use of sword, sabre, pistol, or other arms against each other, wherever they may be quartered, whether in towns, cities, or villages, in camp, or in garrison.

Every officer or other individual of the army, or belonging to it, who shall be convicted of

who have been offended in point of honour to have recourse to the Marshals of France, or their Lieutenants, for reparation, and it inflicts very severe penalties; infamy, loss of nobility, and even death.

having fought a duel shall be shot, as a rebel against the King, a violator of justice, and a disturber of the public peace.

"When two officers, or other individuals of the army, or belonging to it, shall be convicted of fighting in a duel, and that the aggressor cannot be discovered, they shall both be punished according to the above article; but if in the course of the proceeding the aggressor is discovered, then the punishment shall fall upon him only.

"Any officer or other person who shall be convicted of having acted as second, or even third person in a duel, and to have repaired to the place appointed for that purpose, in order to assist or sanction a duel, shall be considered as those already designated, and shall be shot accordingly."*

It is not in England alone, that the voice of reason has been of late raised, for the suppression of this practice, for we find, that the Academy of Arts, Sciences, and Belles-Lettres, at Dijon, have put the following question: the prize to be awarded in 1820 to him who shall give the most satisfactory answer.—"What may be the most effectual means of extirpating from

* Code Henri, loi pénale Militaire, Section 10.

the hearts of Frenchmen that moral disease, a remnant of the barbarism of the middle ages, that false point of honour which leads them to shed blood in duels, in defiance of the precepts of religion and the laws of the state?"— We also find a Bill has been passed by the legislature of Alabama, which subjects the parties engaged in a duel, to three months imprisonment and a fine of two thousand dollars; the offender to give security for his good behaviour for two years, and to be disqualified from holding any office in the state, and from being a Member of either house of the General Assembly." This Bill also requires every officer of the state to take an oath that he has not, since the passing of this act, violated its provisions, and that he will not, during his continuance therein.

The truth is but too obvious, to require further illustration here, that man is wholly and throughout, but a patched and motley composition; and that even the laws of justice themselves, cannot subsist without some mixture of injustice: insomuch, that Plato says, "they undertake to cut off the Hydra's head, who pretend to purge the laws of all inconvenience." Every great example of justice has in it some mixture of injustice, which recompenses the wrong done to particular men, by its public utility; and I think I may assure myself of the concurrence of all good men, in the opinion, that duelling may be restrained by law, if not entirely abolished, without any detriment or interruption to that suavity of manners, which makes the intercourse between man and man in polished society so respectful and agreeable; for though I do admit the influence of this wicked practice over the minds, and actions, of the insolent and the brutish, I cannot suffer myself to be hurried away with the erroneous opinion of its beneficial operation upon men of a different stamp: if therefore inconvenience must be encountered in the suppression of this vice, it is no more than what is in common with all existing laws, which, from the imperfection of our nature, are, and ever must be, defective.

Omniscience belongs not to the wisest, and the best of human governments; in the complex machinery for the suppression of public iniquitous practices, errors do creep in; and thus may our best enacted laws fall short in their operation, in the attainment of the whole end for which they were promulgated. Should it be advanced, that the existing laws for the punishment of murder, are sufficient for the suppression of duelling—to those I would reply, that for the punishment, it may be found adequate, but for the *prevention* of this practice, the present law seems to hold out no intimidation. Instances might be enumerated to infinity in support of this opinion; and were further illustration necessary, the recent trial of the Brittlebanks, at the Derby Assizes, would supply it.

To disarm criticism, I have only, I hope, to remind my Readers — that this work purports to be the production of a young British Officer, who writes not for fame—but with a view to hold up this moral leprosy — duelling — for legislative investigation.

CONTENTS.

	Page
Dedication..................................	iii
Preface.....................................	ix
Preliminary Observations	1
A Brief Display of the Origin and History of Ordeals, &c............................	7
Chap. I. On the Origin and History of Ordeals	
II. On the Origin and History of Trial by Single Combat, or Duel...........	25
III. Trial by Single Combat, in cases of Civil Right...........................	29
IV. Trial by Single Combat, in Appeals of Felony.......................	36
V. Court of Chivalry, or Honour.........	40
VI. Decision of Private Quarrels by Single Combat.......................	45
General Observations, with curious Calculations on the Results of Duels...........	49

DUELS.

1. Between Earl Talbot and John Wilkes, Esq.
2. ...... Mr. Wilkes and Mr. Martin.
3. ...... Mr. Pledger and a Naval Officer.
4. ...... Cornet Gardiner and Rev. Mr. Hill.
5. ...... Lord Byron and William Chaworth, Esq.
6. ...... Lord Kilmaurs and a French Officer.
7. ...... Captain J. and Major A.
8. ...... Major H——th and Lieutenant H.

CONTENTS.

Duel.
9. ...... Between Sieur Chelais and Sieur Reguin.
10. ...... Henry Flood and James Agar, Esqrs.
11. ...... George Garrick, Esq. and Mr. Baddeley.
12. ...... Lord Milton and Lord Poulett.
13. ...... Mr. M'Lean and Mr. Cameron.
14. ...... Marquis de Fleury and an Officer of Distinction.
15. ...... Richard Brinsley Sheridan, Esq. and Mr. Mathews.
16. ...... Lord Townsend and the Earl of Bellamont.
17. ...... Mr. Scawen and Mr. Fitzgerald.
18. ...... Mr. Whateley and John Temple, Esq.
19. ...... Captain Stoney and Reverend Mr. Bate.
20. ...... Count Rice and Viscount du Barry.
21. ...... Lieutenant Col. and Lieutenant of Militia.
22. ...... Honourable Charles James Fox and Mr. Adam.
23. ...... Counsellor R —— and ——.
24. ...... Earl of Shelburne and Colonel Fullarton.
25. ...... Mr. Donovan and Captain James Hanson.
26. ...... Reverend Mr. Bate and Mr. R.
27. ...... Reverend Mr. Allen and Lloyd Dulany, Esq.
28. ...... Duel prevented.
29. ...... Mr. Riddell and Mr. Cunningham.
30. ...... Captain J. and Colonel P.
31. ...... Honorable Colonel Cosmo Gordon and Lieutenant Colonel Thomas.
32. ...... Mr. Monro and Mr. Green.
33. ...... Lieut. Harrison and M. Harman Van Berkensham.
34. ...... Sir James Lowther and Sergeant Bolton.
35. ...... Naval Officer and German Officer.
36. ...... Captain Brises and Captain Bulkley.
37. ...... Lieutenant F. and Mr. Gordon.
38. ...... Lord Macartney and Mr. Sadleir.

CONTENTS.   xxxix.

Duel.
39. Between The Earl of A. and Mr. F. M.
40. ...... Comte de Gersdorff and Monsieur Louis de Favre.
41. ...... Lord William Murray and Mr. Gilbert Waugh.
42. ...... Lieutenants Gamble and Mollison.
43. ...... Lord Macartney and Major General Stewart.
44. ...... Counsellor Hutchinson and Lord Mountmorris.
45. ...... Chevalier La B. and Captain S.
46. ...... Sir John Macpherson and Major Browne.
47. ...... Robert Keon, Esq. and George Nugent Reynolds, Esq.
48. ...... H. R. H. the Duke of York and Colonel Lenox.
49. ...... Captain Edward Pellew and Lieutenant J. M. Northey.
50. ...... Captain Tongue and Captain Paterson.
51. ...... Colonel Lenox and Theophilus Swift, Esq.
52. ...... Mr. Curran, M. P. and Major Hobart.
53. ...... Sir George Ramsay and Captain Macrae.
54. ...... Mr. Stephens and Mr. Anderson.
55. ...... Captain Harvey Aston and Lieutenant Fitzgerald.
56. ...... Mr. Graham and Mr. Julius.
57. ...... Mr. Frizell and Mr. Clarke.
58. ...... Mr. Kemble and Mr. Aikin.
59. ...... Earl of Lonsdale and Captain Cuthbert.
60. ...... Lord Lauderdale and General Arnold.
61. ...... Mons. Chauvigny and Mons. C. Lameth.
62. ...... Mr. Purefoy and Colonel Roper.
63. ...... Major Sweetman and Captain Watson.
64. ...... Mr. Richard England and Mr. Rowlls.
65. ...... Lord Malden and the Duke of Norfolk.

CONTENTS.

Duel.
66. Between Lord Valentia and Henry Gawler, Esq.
67. ...... Mr. Wm. Carpenter and Mr. John Pride.
68. ...... Lieut. Fitzgerald and Lieut. Warrington.
69. ...... Captain Smith and Lieut. Francis Buckley.
70. ...... Colonel King and Colonel Fitzgerald.
71. ...... Right Hon. William Pitt and George Tierney, Esq.
72. ...... Colonel Harvey Aston and Major Allen.
73. ...... Messrs. Coulan and Morcan.
74. ...... James Corry, Esq .and —— Newburgh, Esq.
75. ...... Lieut. B. and Mr. F.
76. ...... Mr. P. Hamilton and Mr. G. I. Eaker.
77. ...... William Hunter, Esq. and Mr. David Mitchell.
78. ...... Lieut. W., Royal Navy, and Captain J. of the Army.
79. ...... Colonel Montgomery and Captain Macnamara.
80. ...... Lord Camelford and Captain Best.
81. ...... The Hon. Aaron Burr and Gen. Hamilton.
82. ...... Ensign Brown and Lieut. Butler.
83. ...... Major Brookes and Colonel Bolton.
84. ...... Lieut. Turrens and Mr. Fisher.
85. ...... Baron Hompesch and Mr. Richardson.
86. ...... Mr. Rogers and Mr. Long.
87. ...... Sir Francis Burdett and Mr. Paull.
88. ...... Lieutenants T. and R.
89. ...... Mr. Arthur Smith and Mr. Thomas Huston.
90. ...... Major Campbell and Captain Boyd.
91. ...... Lord Paget and the Hon. Captain Cadogan.
92. ...... Lord Castlereagh and Mr. Canning.
93. ...... Mr. George Payne and Mr. Clark.
94. ...... Captain Boardman and Ensign de Betton.
95. ...... Mr. Harrison and ——
96. ...... Lieutenant Blundell, 101st Reg. and Mr. Maguire, 6th W. I. Reg.

CONTENTS. xli

Duel.
97. Between Lieut. Stewart and Lieut. Bagnall.
98. ...... Mr. O'Connell and Mr. D'Estree.
99. ...... Colonel Quentin and Colonel Palmer.
100. ...... Mr. ——— and Mr. ———.
101. ...... P. Dillon, Esq. and B Kane, Esq.
102. ...... Mr. Alley and Mr. Adolphus.
103. ...... Major Lockyer and Mr. Sutton Cochrane.
104. ...... Mr. Theodore O'Callaghan and Lieut. Bailey.
105. ...... Lieut. Cartwright and Lieut. Maxwell.
106. ...... Captain N. and Lieut. L———.
107. ...... Captain F-r-b-- and G. R. R———k, Esq.
108. ...... Lieut. Gordon and a French Officer, at Cambray.
109. ...... Lieut. Pickford and Mons. Mariner.
110. ...... Mr. M——— and Mr. B—n.
111. ...... Captain Dobbyn and Mr. Fellowes.
112. ...... Lieut. Williams, R. N. and Mr. Walcot.
113. ...... The Count of C———hee and Major Macintosh.
114. ...... Dr. Bacon and Dr. John S. Hardaway.
115. ...... Mr. Wallace and Mr. Vanhomright.
116. ...... Mr. Searle and Mr. Purver.
117. ...... Mr. Luke White and Captain Conally
118. ...... Lieut. Rodwell, R. N. and Mr. Frame.
119. ...... Mr. Hillson and Mr. Marsden.
120. ...... Mr. B——— and Mr. W———.
121. ...... Duel prevented.
122. ...... Sir J. G. Egerton and Lord Belgrave.
123. ...... The Earl of H——— and Lord W———
124. ...... Mr. H-e-y and Captain E-n-n.
125. ...... F. A. R—n, Esq. and Mr. F—mer.
126. ...... General Mason and Mr. Mac Carty.
127. ...... Captain Johnston, 64th Reg. and Benjamin T. Browne, Surgeon of the American sloop of war Erie.

d

Duel.
128. Between Captain Freeth, 64th Regiment, and Mr. Montgomery, American sloop Erie.
129. ...... C. J. Allingham, Esq. and J. O'Neil, Esq.
130. ...... Lieut. L-l-a-s and P. R. M-i-g, Esq.
131. ...... Captain Kirsopp and W. Payton, Esq.
132. ...... Mr. Uniacke and Mr. Bowie.
133. ...... Lieut. P—— and Capt. D——.
134. ...... Captain Hussey and Lieut. Osborn, both 38th Reg.
135. ...... Charles Phillips, Esq. and ——Henriques, Esq.
136. ...... Two Naval Officers, Hakens and Frazer.
137. ...... Captain Pellew, 1st Life Guards, and Lieut. Walsh.
138. ...... Captain S—— and Mr. Baring.
139. ...... Captain W—— and a French Gentleman.
140. ...... Colonel D—— and Captain M——.
141. ...... F. S. W-t-h, Esq. and Captain H—s.
142. ...... D. F—ll, Esq. and B. F—n, Esq.
143. ...... Captain H-n-u and Mr. B-e-r.
144. ...... Mr. F—— and Mr. S——.
145. ...... Lieut. J. C. Smith, 27th Reg. and Lieut. Dowling, American Navy.
146. ...... The Hon. Christopher Hely Hutchinson and Patrick W. Callaghan, Esq.
147. ...... C. S. W-ll-ce and W. S——d, Esq.
148. ...... Mr. Grattan and Lord Clare.
149. ...... Captain F—w and Mr. G—y.
150. ...... Mr. E——d, and Mr. R—t—d.
151. ...... T. Hungerford, Esq. and R. Travers, Esq.
152. ...... Mr. R. Stewart and Mr. T. S. Dade.
153. ...... Mr. Fulliot and Mr. Burrowes.
154. ...... Mr. Fenshaw and Mr. Hartinger.
155. ...... Captain T-r-t and Mr. S——.
156. ...... Colonel W-ls-n and Mr. J——s.

CONTENTS. xliii

Duel.
157. Between Mr. M——a and Mr. C——g.
158. ...... Mr. H——n and Mr. S-y-r.
159. ...... Captain J——, Royal Navy, and Mr. H——.
160. ...... —— Brown, Esq. and —— Gresham, Esq.
161. ...... Major D——m and Mr. M-r-n.
162. ...... Mr. John Scott and Mr. Christie.
163. ...... R. Gough, Esq. and Lieutenant Colonel Camac, 1st Life Guards
164. ...... Mr. F-l-d and Mr. M-s-n.
165. ...... M. Manuel and M. Beaumont, at Paris.
166. ...... Captain S—— and Captain A——, Royal Artillery.
167. ...... Mr. C-m-y and Captain Fo-r-r.
168. ...... Lord Petersham and Mr. W. Wedderburn.
169. ...... Major Ogilvie, 4th Dragoons, and Capt. P. Browne, South Mayo Militia.
170. ...... Mr. W. Brittlebank and Mr. Cuddie.
171. ...... Major G—— and Major T——.
172. ...... Captain T—— and Mr. R——.

PRELIMINARY OBSERVATIONS.

MAN, in his individual, or aggregate character, alike presents an exhaustless subject of political and moral disquisition. The talents of his mind, and the passions of his heart, open a field of observation, which cannot fail to excite the most powerful, and, at the same time, the most contradictory sensations. For, if we select from the mass of our associates any distinguished individual, and analyze the whole of his intellect, the whole of his moral qualities, the whole of his character — what object do we present to the critical examination of our judgment?—A being, possibly, of high intellectual endowments, but marked by the most ridiculous prejudices; the possessor of great moral qualities, united with the most debasing habits: a character, in short, of a compound nature, enjoying talents and habits, that excite, at once, our admiration and contempt, our reverence and disgust.

If with the same critical eye we look at communities of men, as presented to us in the interesting records of faithful and philosophical historians, do we not, on this more enlarged theatre of investigation, perceive the operation of the same contending principles? Even in regard to the most polished nations, both of ancient and modern times, is not our admiration raised by the sublimity of some of their institutes; the comprehensive and liberal nature of some of their social principles — and our disgust, in an equal degree, excited by the disgraceful origin and injurious effects of others? Instances, including affirmative answers to these important enquiries, might be multiplied almost to infinity, even from the annals of the most civilized communities. The number, in one scale at least, and that not the most honourable to the proud intellect of man, would, doubtless, be extended, were the appeal made to the records of nations less enlightened, less favoured by intellectual, moral, and political improvement.

The generous and ardent friend of his species may exercise his benevolent wish, that mankind, both individually and collectively may, in process of time, present a greater uniformity in intellectual and in moral excellence. And the political theorist, in union with the ethical writer, may, in the mean time, usefully employ his talents and experience in ingenious attempts to realize this desideratum in the speculative field of human happiness.

It is the object of the present Work, to mark the imbecility and inconsistency of man in one of the principal features of his individual and collective character. And a train of peculiar circumstances has placed this difficult and delicate subject in hands not much accustomed to an office of such nicety and importance. It is most willingly acknowledged, that, by an abler and more experienced writer, it might have been rendered more highly interesting, by presenting materials of sufficient importance to stimulate some powerful and highly-gifted friend of his country, to institute enquiries, to prepare and mature principles, and plans for the legislative removal of those evils, which, even in these enlightened days, still attach to the unrivalled system of English Jurisprudence.

If, however, it should, even under these acknowledged disadvantages, prove instrumental in realizing, in a small degree, the wishes of the benevolent; if it should tend to purify the institutes, and eventually the characters of men, and thus lessen the number of human victims, which might, otherwise, be sacrificed on polluted altars, the Author conceives that he could rejoice in sweetening the full cup of sorrows, which the operation of an evil custom has presented to the lips of too many at a very early period in life, and which they have been compelled to drink to the very lees. It may, probably, soften the melancholy feelings which past recollections of ill-treatment have necessarily rendered familiar to the minds of military men, and console them, by producing a conviction, that their sufferings have been of some benefit to their countrymen, and particularly to that valuable profession, to which, in their early outset, they had attached the most brilliant enjoyments of life; every thing that in their fascinated and youthful mind was calculated to rouze, to exercise, to invigorate, and to mature the principles, the feelings, and the characteristic honour of British soldiers.

Without farther preface, or preliminary discussion, the Author now solicits the Reader's attention to the contents of the following chapters, which will include a brief outline of a subject, which he conceives of no mean moment to the intellectual, political, and moral character of Englishmen.

CHAPTER I.

ON THE ORIGIN AND GENERAL HISTORY OF ORDEALS.

ORDEAL was an appeal to the immediate interposition of Divine Power, and was peculiarly distinguished by the appellation of " Judicium Dei," the *Judgment of God;* and sometimes " Vulgaris Purgatio," the *Common Purgation;* to distinguish it from the *Canonical Purgation,* which was by the oath of the party. There were in Europe two kinds of it more common than the rest; namely, Fire Ordeal and Water Ordeal. The former was confined to persons of *higher rank;* the latter to the *common people.* Both these might be performed by deputy: but the principal was to answer for the success of the trial; the deputy only venturing some bodily penalty for hire, or, probably, volunteering his services from a principle of friendship.

That the purgation by Ordeal of some species or other, is very ancient, admits of no doubt; and that it was universal, in times of superstitious barbarity, is equally certain. It appears, also, to have been known, and practised, among the ancient Greeks. For, in the "Antigone," of Sophocles, a person suspected by Creon of a misdemeanor, declares himself ready to "handle hot iron, and to walk over fire," in order to manifest his innocence: which, the scholiast tells us, was then a very usual purgation. And Grotius communicates many instances of *Water Ordeal*, in Bythinia, Sardinia, and other countries.

It appears, however, to have prevailed to a greater extent among the Hindoos than among any other people; for, in a paper of the "Asiatic Researches," communicated by the celebrated Warren Hastings, Esq. we find that the "trial by Ordeal," among them, is conducted in *nine* different ways.

1. By the Balance. 2. By Fire. 3. By Water. 4. By Poison. 5. By Cosha, or Water in which an idol has been washed. 6. By Rice. 7. By boiling Oil. 8. By red hot Iron. 9. By Images.

1. Ordeal by the "Balance," is thus performed. The beam, having been previously

adjusted, the cord fixed, and both scales made perfectly even, the person accused, and a Pandit, fast a whole day. Then, after the accused has been bathed in sacred water, the homa, or oblation, presented to Fire, and the deities worshipped, he is carefully weighed; and when he is taken out of the scale, the Pandits prostrate themselves before it, pronounce a certain mentra or incantation, agreeably to the Sastras, and having written the substance of the accusation on a piece of paper, bind it on his head. Six minutes after, they place him again in the scale, and if he weigh more than before, he is held guilty; if less, innocent; if exactly the same, he must be weighed a third time; when, as it is written in the Mitacshera, there will certainly be a difference in his weight. Should the balance, though well fixed, break down, this would be considered as a proof of his guilt.

2. For the purpose of performing the " Fire Ordeal," an excavation, nine hands long, two spans broad, and one span deep, is made in the ground, and filled with a fire of pippal wood. Into this the person accused must walk bare-footed; and if his

foot be unhurt, they hold him blameless; if burned, guilty.

3. The "Water Ordeal" is performed by causing the person accused to stand in a certain depth of water, either flowing or stagnant, to reach his navel; but care is to be taken, that no ravenous beast be in it; and, that it be not moved by much air. A Brachman is then directed to go into the water, holding a staff in his hand; and a soldier shoots three arrows on dry ground from a bow of cane. A man is then dispatched to bring the arrow that has been shot the farthest; and, after he has taken it up, another is ordered to run from the edge of the water; at which instant, the person accused is told to grasp the foot, or the staff, of the Brachman, who stands near him in the water, and immediately to dive into it. He must remain under water, till the two men, who went to fetch the arrows, are returned. For, if he raise his head, or body, above the surface, before the arrows are brought back, his guilt is considered as fully proved. In the villages near Benares, it is the practice for the person to be tried by this kind of ordeal, to stand in water up

to his navel; and, then, holding the foot of a Brachman, to dive under it as long as a man can walk fifty paces very gently. If, before the man has walked thus far, the accused rise above the water, he is condemned: if not, acquitted.

A very peculiar species of "Water Ordeal" is said to prevail among the Indians on the Coast of Malabar. A person accused of an enormous crime is obliged to swim over a large river, abounding with crocodiles; and, if he escape unhurt, he is esteemed innocent.

At Siam, besides the usual modes of "Fire, and Water Ordeal," both parties are exposed to the fury of a tiger, let loose upon them for that purpose; and if the beast spares either, that person is accounted innocent: if neither, both are held to be guilty: but, if he spares both, the trial is incomplete, and they proceed to a more certain criterion.

4. There are two sorts of "Trial by Poison;"—First, the Pandits having performed their homa, and the accused person his ablution, two rettis and a half, or seven barleycorns, of Vishanaga, a poisonous root,

or of Sanc'hya, that is, white arsenic, are mixed in eight mashas, or sixty-four rettis, of clarified butter, which the accused must eat from the hand of a Brachman. If the poison produces no visible effect, he is absolved; otherwise, he is condemned. Second, The hooded snake, called Naga, is thrown into a deep earthen pot, into which is dropped a ring, a seal, or a coin. This the accused person is ordered to take out with his hand; and if the serpent bite him, he is pronounced guilty; if not, innocent.

5. The " Trial by Cosha" is as follows: The accused is made to drink three drafts of the water, in which the images of the Sun, Devi, and other Deities, have been washed for that purpose; and if, within fourteen days, he has any sickness, or indisposition, his crime is considered as proved.

6. When several persons are suspected of theft, some dry rice is weighed with the sacred stone called Salgram, or certain slocas are read over it: after which, the suspected persons are severally ordered to chew a quantity of it. As soon as they have chewed it, they are to throw it on

some leaves of pippal, or, if none be at hand, on some b'hurja patra, or bark of a tree from Nepal or Cashmir. The man, from whose mouth the rice comes dry or stained with blood, is holden guilty. The rest are acquitted.

7. The "Ordeal by hot Oil" is very simple. It is thus performed. The ground appointed for the trial is cleared, and rubbed with cow-dung; and the next day at sun-rise, the Pandit worships Ganisa, or the Hindoo Janus, presents his oblations, and pays adoration to other deities, conformably to the Sastra. Then, having read the incantation prescribed, he places a round pan of gold, silver, copper, iron, or clay, with a diameter of sixteen fingers, and four fingers deep, and throws into it one sér, or eighty sicca weight, of clarified butter, or oil of sesamum. After this, a ring of gold, or silver, or iron, is cleaned and washed with water, and cast into the oil, which they proceed to heat, and when it is very hot, put into it a fresh leaf of pippala, or of bilua. When the leaf is burned, the oil is known to be sufficiently hot. Then, having pronounced a mentra over the oil, they order

the party accused, to take the ring out of the pan; and, if he take it out without being burned, or without a blister on his hand, his innocence is considered as proved; if not, his guilt.

8. In the same manner, they make an iron ball or the head of a lance, red hot, and place it in the hands of the person accused, who, if it burn him not, is judged guiltless.

9. To perform the ordeal by Dharm'arch, which is the name of the sloca appropriated to this mode of trial, either an image, named Dharma, or the Genius of Justice, is made of silver, and another, called Adharma, of clay or iron, both of which are thrown into a large earthen jar; and the accused having thrust his hand into it, is acquitted, if he bring out the silver image; but condemned, if he draw forth the iron. Or, the figure of a deity is painted on white cloth, and another on black; the first of which they name Dharma, and the second Adharma. These are severally rolled up in cow-dung, and thrown into a large jar, without having been shewn to the accused, who must put his hand into the jar, and is

acquitted or convicted, as he draws out the figure on white or on black cloth.

In Europe, the Fire Ordeal was performed either by taking up in the hand, unhurt, a piece of red-hot iron, of one, two, or three pounds weight; or else, by walking, barefoot, and blindfold, over nine red-hot ploughshares, laid lengthwise, at unequal distances: and if the party escaped being burned, he was adjudged innocent. But if it happened otherwise, as, without collusion, it usually did, he was then condemned as guilty. However, by this latter method, Emma, the mother of Edward the Confessor, is mentioned to have cleared her character, when suspected of familiarity with Alwyn, Bishop of Winchester.

The first account we have of the appeal of Christians to the "Fire Ordeal," as a proof of their innocence, is that of Simplicius, Bishop of Autun, who lived in the fourth century. This prelate, as the story is related, before his promotion to the episcopal order, had married a wife, who loved him tenderly, and who, unwilling to quit him after his advancement, continued to sleep in the same chamber with him. The sanctity of Simplicius suffered, at least in the voice of fame, by the constancy of his wife's affection: and it was rumoured, that the holy man, though a bishop, persisted, in opposition to the canonical laws, to taste the sweets of matrimony; upon which his wife, in the presence of a great concourse of people, took up a considerable quantity of burning coals, which she held in her clothes, and applied to her breasts, without the least hurt, as the legend says, to her person or her garments. And her example being followed by her husband with similar success, the silly multitude admired the miracle, and proclaimed the innocence of the loving pair. A similar trick was played by St. Brice in the fifth century.*

In Europe, "Water Ordeal" was performed, either by plunging the bare arm up to the elbow in boiling water; or, by casting the person suspected into a river, or pond, of cold water; and if he floated therein, without any action of swimming, it was deemed an evidence of his guilt; but if he sunk, he was acquitted. It is easy to trace out the traditional relics of this water

* Mosheim's Ecclesiastical History, Vol. II.

ordeal, in the ignorant barbarity, still practised in many countries to discover witches, by casting them into a pool of water, and drowning them to prove their innocence.

Thus is the superstitious weakness of mankind most astonishing. There is nothing too absurd for them to profess as an article of belief, nor too impious to reduce into their practice. Nor can the truth of this position be made more obvious, than by referring to the Trial by Ordeal. The gross absurdity, as well as impiety, of pronouncing a man guilty, unless cleared by a miracle, and of expecting that all the powers of nature should be suspended, by an immediate interposition of Providence to save the innocent, whenever it was presumptuously required, is self-evident. Yet its origin may be attributable to necessity, as well as superstition. At the period of its origin in England, as well as in other countries of Europe, it was no easy matter for an innocent person, when accused of guilt, to prove his innocence by the established modes of trial. It was, therefore, to be expected, that superstition would fly to Heaven for those testimonies of innocence, which the absurdity of human laws frequently prevented men from obtaining in the ordinary way. It is doubtless, that in this combined principle the "Trial by Ordeal" commenced; and what was begun by necessitous superstition, was fostered and prolonged by impious and selfish priestcraft and unjust power. During all the processes of these ridiculous trials, there was a wide field for delusion and deceit; and there can be no question that it was often practised.

Besides those particular methods of trial which have been already mentioned, there were others more common in European countries, as: the Judicial Combat, which forms the subject of the succeeding chapter; the Ordeal of the Cross, and the Ordeal of the Corsned.

It was so much the custom in the middle ages of Christianity to respect the Cross, even to superstition, that it would indeed have been wonderful, if the ignorant bigotry of the times had not converted it into an ordeal. We accordingly find it used for this purpose in so many different ways, as almost to preclude description. The following account is given of this ordeal, and that of the Corsned, by Doctor Henry.

"In criminal trials the judgment of the Cross was commonly thus conducted. When the prisoner had declared his innocence upon oath, and appealed to the judgment of the Cross, two sticks were prepared exactly like one another; the figure of the Cross was cut on one of these sticks, and nothing on the other. Each of them was then wrapped up in a quantity of fine white wool, and laid on the altar, or on the relics of the saints; after which, a solemn prayer was put up to God, that he would be pleased to discover, by evident signs, whether the prisoner were innocent or guilty. This solemnity being finished, a priest approached the altar, and took up one of the sticks, which was uncovered with much anxiety. If it was the stick marked with the cross, the prisoner was pronounced innocent; if it was the other, he was declared guilty.

"When the judgment of the Cross was appealed to in civil cases, the trial proceeded thus. The judges, parties, and all concerned, being assembled in a church, each of the parties chose a priest, the youngest and stoutest he could find, to be his representative in the trial. These representatives were then placed, one on each side of some famous crucifix; and at a signal given, they both at once stretched their arms at full length, so as to form a cross with their bodies. In this painful posture they continued to stand while Divine Service was performing; and the party, whose representative dropped his arm first, lost his cause.

"The Corsned, or the consecrated bread and cheese, was the ordeal to which the clergy commonly appealed when they were accused of any crime; in which they acted a very prudent part, as it was attended with no danger or inconvenience. This ordeal was performed in the following manner. A piece of barley bread and a piece of cheese were laid upon the altar, over which a priest pronounced certain conjurations, and prayed with great fervency, that if the accused was guilty, God would send his angel Gabriel to stop his throat, that he might not be able to swallow that bread and cheese. These prayers being ended, the culprit approached the altar, took up the bread and cheese, and began to eat it. If he swallowed freely, he was declared innocent; but if it stuck in his throat, and he could not swallow (which we may presume seldom or never happened), he was pronounced guilty."

Besides these, various other ordeals were practised in christian countries, many of which retain the same names as among the Pagans, and differ only in the mode of execution. In all the nations of Christians in which those trials were used, we find that the clergy were engaged in them. Indeed in England so late as the time of King John, we find grants to the bishops and clergy, to use the " Judicium ferri, aquæ, et ignis ;" the " trial of iron, water, and fire." And both in England and Sweden the clergy presided at these trials, and they were only performed in the churches and other consecrated ground. But to give the canon law its due praise, we find it very early declaring against trial by ordeal, as being the " Fabric of the Devil." Upon this authority, though the canons themselves were of no validity in England, it was thought proper, (as had been done in Denmark above a century before), to disuse and abolish this trial entirely in our courts of justice, by an act of Parliament in 3 Henry III. according to Sir Edward Coke.

It may here be enquired how the effects of these trials were evaded? and how it was possible to appear to do, what we know could not be really done, without material injury to the persons concerned? And this part of the subject is so well treated by the learned historian, who has been already quoted, that this article cannot be better finished than in his own words.

" If we suppose that few, or none, escaped conviction, who exposed themselves to these trials, we shall be very much mistaken; for the histories of those times contain innumerable examples of persons, plunging their naked arms into boiling water, handling red-hot balls of iron, and walking upon burning ploughshares, without receiving the least injury. Many learned men have been much puzzled to account for this, and disposed to think, that Providence graciously interposed in a miraculous manner for the preservation of injured innocence. But if we examine every circumstance of those fiery trials with due attention, we shall see sufficient reason to suspect that the whole was a gross imposition on the credulity of mankind. The accused person was committed wholly to the priest, who was to perform the ceremony, three days before the trial, in which he had time enough to bargain with him for his deliverance, and give him instruction how to act his part. On the day of trial, no person was allowed to enter the church but the priest and the accused, till after the iron was heated; when, twelve friends of the accusers, and twelve of the accused, and no more, were admitted, and arranged along the wall, at each side of the church, at a respectful distance. After the iron was taken out of the fire, several prayers were said; the accused drank a cup of holy water, and sprinkled his hands with it, which might take a considerable time, if the priest were indulgent. The space of nine feet was measured by the accused himself with his own feet, and he would probably give but scanty measure. He was obliged only to touch one of the marks with the toe of his right foot, and allowed to stretch the other foot as far towards the other mark as he could; so that the conveyance was almost instantaneous. His hand was not immediately examined, but wrapped in a cloth, prepared for that purpose, three days. May we not, then, from all these precautions suspect, that these priests were in possession of some secret that secured the hand from the impression of such a momentary touch of hot iron, or removed all appearances of these impressions in three days, and that they made use of this secret when they saw reason? What greatly strengthens this suspicion is, that we meet with no example of any champion of the Romish Church, who suffered the least injury from the touch of hot iron in this ordeal. But, when any one was so fool-hardy, as to appeal to it, or to that of hot water, with a view to deprive the church of any of her possessions, *he never failed to burn his fingers*, and lose his cause."

CHAPTER II.

ON THE ORIGIN, AND GENERAL HISTORY OF TRIAL BY SINGLE COMBAT, OR DUEL.

In the modern and common acceptation, the term 'Duel' signifies a single combat originating in a feeling of personal offence, and followed by a regular Cartel, or challenge, fixing a time and place, mutually convenient to the combatants. These individuals are termed principals, and are usually accompanied to the field, by two gentlemen, in the quality of friends, or seconds, for the purpose of arranging, and superintending, all the preliminaries, and proceedings of the combat.

But this view of the practice, comprehends only that branch of it, which is retained by more modern times. At an earlier period, it constituted an important part of the common law in those realms, in which it prevailed. In this view, Fleta defines a duel in the following terms. " Singularis pugna est inter duos, ad probandum veritatis litis; et qui vicit, probasse intelligitur." It is a single combat, for the purpose of ascertaining to whom the principle of right belongs, in a disputed point; and he who conquers, does by that act, justify and establish his claim.

In a rude age, and amongst a superstitious and weak race of men, there is no just cause to marvel, that such an appeal should originate and prevail. And accordingly, we find that it sprung from the barbarous hordes of the north, on the assumption, that God would never grant the victory in these cases, but to the man who had the best right.

The trial by duel, then, was obviously a method, instituted for the purpose of consulting Providence in all disputed cases of CIVIL RIGHT—of learning, also, in *criminal transactions*, who was, in truth, the offending party; and it was conjectured, and even confidently supposed, that the deity, thus interrogated, would not fail to support all just claims; to give countenance to the innocent, and to confound the guilty: for it was admitted by this appeal, that the right of the case was perceived by an Omniscient eye, though concealed from human penetration.

Thus, in the absence of those enlightened principles, which are connected with just views of the universe, and of its great Governor, and which are in perpetual enmity with superstition in all its forms, did this barbarous and insensate usage prevail throughout the greatest part of civilized Europe. For, towards the close of the fifth century, it was introduced into Italy by the Lombards; and, in course of time, became an established law in Germany, Denmark, Gaul, and the rest of Europe. In consequence of its prevalence amongst the Franks and Normans, its introduction into England was a matter of course, when William of Normandy secured his claim to the throne of this country, by the successful battle of Hastings.*

There were three cases only, in which this mode of trial was adopted in England, viz.

* The day before the battle of Hastings, William sent an offer to Harold to decide their quarrel by single combat, and thus to spare the blood of thousands; but Harold refused, saying, he would leave it to the God of Armies to determine. The next day, October 14th, 1066, victory declared in favour of William.

1. Civil, upon issue joined in a writ of right.

2. Criminal, as in appeals of felony.

3. Military, as exhibited in the Court Martial, or Court of Chivalry, and Honour.

In the following chapters, the reader's attention is called to the particulars of each case.

CHAPTER III.

TRIAL BY SINGLE COMBAT, IN CASES OF CIVIL RIGHT.

This was the only mode of decision of writs of right, from the time of William of Normandy, until that of Henry II. who, with the consent of Parliament, introduced the alternative of the grand assize, or the trial by Jury.

It often happened that in these writs of right, the ' Jus Proprietatis,' or the right of property, could not be ascertained, without great difficulty. The mode of determining by battle was, therefore, resorted to on behalf of those claimants, who might possess the true right; but, who yet, in consequence of the death of witnesses, or other accidental, or unavoidable defects of evidence, were unable to prove that right to a Jury. Although the writ of right itself, and of consequence this stupid, and disgraceful mode of trial, be so far disused, as to be considered as nearly obsolete, yet the law is not abrogated, and is, therefore, still in force, if the parties concerned choose to abide by it.

The last trial by Battle, which was waged in the Court of Common Pleas at Westminster, took place in the thirteenth year of Queen Elizabeth, 1571, and was held in Tothill Fields. Sir Henry Spelman gives an account of it, being an eye-witness of the whole ceremony, and says, that it was conducted, " Non sine magna Juris-consultorum perturbatione." Not without great disturbance amongst the gentlemen of the Long Robe. One, however, afterwards occurred in the Court of Chivalry in 1631; and another in the County Palatine of Durham in 1638.

No apology is necessary for the insertion of the form and circumstances, attending this remnant of barbarism. It is given on the authority of Mr. Justice Blackstone, and will, doubtless, make its due impression, when viewed in connection with the interest, which recent occurrences have attached to it, in the case of Thornton and Ashford.

When the tenant, in a writ of right, pleads the general issue, viz. that he hath more right to hold, than the demandant hath to recover, and offers to prove it by the body of his champion, which tender is accepted by the demandant; the tenant, in the first place, must produce his champion, who, by throwing down his glove as a gage or pledge, thus wages, or stipulates, battle, with the champion of the demandant, who, by taking up the glove or gage, stipulates on his part, to accept the challenge. The reason why it is waged by champions, and not by the parties themselves, in civil actions, is because, if any party to the suit dies, the suit must abate, and be at an end for the present; and, therefore, no judgment could be given for the lands in question, if either of the parties were slain in the battle; and, also, that no person might claim an exemption from this trial, as was allowed in criminal cases, in which the battle was waged in person.

When the preliminaries are thus adjusted, a piece of ground is, in due time, set out, of sixty feet square, inclosed with lists, and on one side a court is erected for the accommodation of the judges of the Court of Common Pleas, who attend there in their scarlet robes. A bar is, also, prepared for the sergeants learned in the law.

When the Court sits, which ought to be before sun-rising, proclamation is made for the parties, and their champions. The latter are introduced by two knights, and are dressed in a coat of armour, with red sandals, bare-legged from the knee downwards, bare-headed, and with bare arms to the elbows. The weapons allowed them are, batons, or staves, of an ell long, and a four-cornered leather target; so that death very seldom ensued from these civil combats. In the Court Military, however, Spelman and Rushworth inform us, that they fought with sword and lance. It appears, also, that in France villeins only fought with the buckler and baton; but that gentlemen were armed at all points. And in adverting to this and other circumstances, the Duke of Sully, and after him the President Montesquieu, has, with great ingenuity, not only deduced the pernicious custom of private duelling upon imaginary points of honour, but has, also, traced the heroic madness of knight-errantry to the same origin, that is, to judicial combats.

When the champions, thus armed with batons, arrive within the lists, or place of combat, the champion of the tenant, then takes his adversary by the hand, and makes oath, that the tenements, in dispute, are not the right of the demandant : and the champion of the demandant, taking the other by the hand, swears in the same manner, that they are. So that each champion is, or ought to be, thoroughly persuaded of the truth of the cause, for which he fights. An oath is then taken against sorcery and enchantment, by both champions, in the following, or similar form :

" Hear this, ye justices, that I have neither eaten, drunk, nor have I upon me either bone, stone, or grass; no enchantment, sorcery, or witchcraft, whereby the law of God may be abased; or the law of the Devil exalted. So help me, God and his Saints !"

The battle is then begun, and the combatants are bound to fight till the stars appear in the evening; and, if the champion of the tenant can defend himself till the stars appear, the tenant shall prevail in his cause ; for it is sufficient for him to maintain his ground, and make it a drawn battle, he being already in possession; but if victory declares itself for either party, for him is judgment finally given. This victory may arise from the death of either of the champions, which has rarely happened, the whole ceremony, though involving consequences of the highest importance, bearing a resemblance to those athletic and rustic diversions, which are not uncommon, and which are probably derived from this origin. Victory is, also, obtained, if either champion proves recreant, that is, yields, and pronounces the word Craven, which is a word of disgrace and obloquy, rather than of any determinate meaning. But it is a term of terrible import to the vanquished champion; since, as a punishment to him, for forfeiting the land of his principal, he is, by pronouncing it, condemned, as a recreant, " Amittere liberam legem," that is, to become infamous, and not to be considered, " Liber et legalis homo;" being supposed, by the event, to be forsworn; and, therefore, in future, not eligible as a juryman, or in a condition to be admitted as a witness in any cause.

This is the form of a trial by battle; a trial, which the tenant or defendant, in a writ of right, has it in his election at this day to demand; and, which was the only decision of such writ of right after the conquest, until the time of Henry II. who, by consent of Parliament, introduced the grand Assize, a peculiar species of trial by jury, in concurrence therewith; giving the tenant his choice of either the one or the other. This example of discountenancing judicial combats was imitated about a century afterwards, in France, by an edict of Louis the Pious A. D. 1260, and soon after by the rest of Europe.

Glanvil, Chief Justice to Henry II. and probably his adviser in this important measure, considers the establishment of this alternative, as a most noble improvement of the law. And in fact so it was, being the commencement of that beneficial process in courts of law, which has constituted the best foundation and security of all public and private right, both in regard to the persons, and properties of individuals.

CHAPTER IV.

TRIAL BY SINGLE COMBAT, IN APPEALS OF FELONY.

The Trial by Battle may be demanded by the appellee, in an appeal of felony. And this process is carried on with equal solemnity as in a writ of right, with this difference, that in the latter, each party might hire a champion; but in appeals of felony, they must fight in their proper persons. And, therefore, if the appellant be a woman, a priest, an infant, or of the age of sixty, or lame, or blind, he, or she, may counterplead, and refuse the wager of battle, and compel the appellee to put himself upon the country. Peers of the realm, also, bringing an appeal, shall not be challenged to wage battle, on account of the dignity of their persons: nor the citizens of London, by special charter, because fighting is considered foreign to their education and employment. So likewise, if the crime be notorious, as, for example, if the thief be taken with the 'manour' (the property,) or the murderer in the room with a bloody knife, the appellant may refuse the tender of battle from the appellee. For it is unreasonable that an innocent man should stake his life against one who is already half convicted.

The form and manner of waging battle in appeals of felony are nearly the same as upon a writ of right. The oaths, however, of the two combatants are more striking and solemn.

The appellee, when appealed of felony, pleads, "Not Guilty," and throws down his glove, declaring that he will defend the same by his body. The appellant takes up the glove, and replies, that he is ready to make good the appeal, body to body. The appellee then taking the Bible in his right hand, and in his left the right hand of his antagonist, swears to this effect: "Hoc audi, homo, quem per manum teneo," &c. &c. &c. "Hear this, O man, whom I hold by the hand, who callest thyself John, by the name of baptism, that I, who call myself Thomas, by the name of baptism, did not feloniously murder thy father, William by name, nor am any way guilty of the said felony; so help me, God, and the saints! and this I will defend against thee by my body, as this court shall award." To which the appellant replies, holding the Bible and his antagonist's hand, in the same manner as the other. " Hear this, O man, whom I hold by the hand, who callest thyself Thomas, by the name of baptism, that thou art perjured ; and, therefore, perjured, because thou feloniously didst murder my father, William by name; so help me, God, and the saints ! and this I will prove against thee by my body, as this court shall award."

The battle is then fought with the same weapons, viz. batons, the same solemnity, and the same oaths against amulets and sorcery, that are used in the civil combat. And if the appellee be so far vanquished that he cannot, or will not, fight any longer, he shall be adjudged to be hanged immediately : and then, as well as if he be killed in battle, Providence is deemed to have determined in favour of the truth, and his blood shall be attainted. The punishment of the vanquished was that which the crime merited of which he was accused. If it were a capital crime the vanquished was disarmed, led out of the field, and immediately executed, together with the party whose cause he had maintained. If the conquered champion fought in the cause of a woman, she was burned.

But if the appellee kills the appellant, or can maintain the fight from sun-rising, till the stars appear in the evening, he shall be acquitted. So, also, if the appellant becomes recreant, and pronounces the word " Craven," he shall lose his " Liberam legem," and become infamous; and the appellee shall recover damages; and, also, be for ever quit, not only of the appeal, but of all indictments for the same offence.

Having laid before the Reader a compressed account of all that is requisite to illustrate the origin, history, and operation of this usage, as it relates to civil and criminal processes, it remains, after devoting a brief chapter to a display of the former jurisdiction and present state of the Court of Chivalry or Honour, to view it in relation to the conduct and decision of private quarrels.

CHAPTER V.

COURT OF CHIVALRY, OR HONOUR.

This Court was formerly held by the Lord High Constable, and Earl Marshal of England jointly, and possessed both a civil and criminal jurisdiction. But since the attainder of Stafford Duke of Buckingham, under Henry VIII. and the consequent extinction of the office of Lord High Constable, it hath usually, with respect to civil matters, been heard by the Earl Marshal only.

This court, by a statute of the Second Richard, hath cognisance of contracts and other matters relative to deeds of arms and war, as well out of the realm as in it; and from its sentence lies an immediate appeal to the King in person. In the times of pure chivalry this court was in great reputation; and afterwards, during the English connection with the continent, in consequence of the territories held by their princes in France. But it has now almost become obsolete, on account of the feebleness of its jurisdiction, and the want of that power which is necessary to enforce its judgments; for, being no court of record, it can neither fine nor imprison.

The civil jurisdiction of the Court of Chivalry had respect to two points: the redress of injuries of honour, and the correction of encroachments in matters of coat armour, precedency and other distinctions of families.

As a Court of Honour, its jurisdiction lies in giving satisfaction to all those who are aggrieved in points of honour, in points, which are of so nice and delicate a nature, as to include wrongs and injuries which escape the notice of the common law, and yet which imperiously require redress of some species. Of this class is the application of the term " coward," to a soldier, and that of " liar," to a gentleman. These opprobrious and insulting terms, though acutely galling to the feelings of an honourable mind, yet, being productive of no immediate damage to the person or property of the individual, no action will lie in the courts at Westminster; and yet they are injuries of such a nature, as will prompt every man of spirit to demand honourable amends, and this amends, by the ancient law of the land, was given in the Court of Chivalry. But modern relations have determined, that however expedient a jurisdiction may be, yet that no action for words is at present cognizable by it; and it hath been always clearly held, that this Court cannot interfere in any matter which is determinable by common law. It can, therefore, give no pecuniary satisfaction or damages, inasmuch as the quantity and determination of it is cognizable only by common law; and, therefore, the Court of Chivalry can, at most, order reparation in points of honour; as, to compel the defendant, " Mendacium sibi ipsi imponere," or, to take to himself the lie which he has given, or, to make such other submission as the laws of honour may require.

The other point of the jurisdiction of this Court lies, in the redress of usurpations and encroachments, in matters of heraldry, and coat armour. It is the business of this Court, according to Sir Matthew Hale, to adjust armorial ensigns, bearings, crests, supporters, pennons, &c. &c. and, also, rights of places and precedence, where the King's Patent, or Act of Parliament, which cannot be over-ruled by this Court, have not already determined. The proceedings in this Court are by petition, in a summary way; and the trial, not by a jury of twelve men, but by witnesses, or by combat. But, as it cannot imprison, not being a court of record; and, as by the resolutions of the superior courts, it is now confined to so narrow and restrained a jurisdiction, it has fallen into contempt. The marshalling of coat armour, which was formerly the pride and study of all the best families in the kingdom, is now greatly disregarded; and has fallen into the hands of certain officers and attendants upon this Court, called Heralds, who consider it only as a matter of profit, and not of justice: the consequence is, that such falsity and confusion have crept into their records (which ought to be the standing evidence of families, descents, and coat armour), that though formerly some credit has been paid to their testimony, now even their common seal will not be received as evidence in any court of justice in the kingdom. But their original visitation books, compiled when progresses were solemnly and regularly made into every part of the kingdom, to enquire into the state of families, and to register such marriages and descents, as were verified to them upon oath, are allowed to be good evidence of pedigrees.

CHAPTER VI.

DECISION OF PRIVATE QUARRELS, BY SINGLE COMBAT.

It is not unreasonable to infer, that men, accustomed to witness the mode of determination adopted in courts of justice, which has been displayed in two of the preceding chapters, would feel no repugnance to the application of it to their private disputes. Accordingly, it happened that personal combats, which originally were appointed, sanctioned, and even conducted by judges alone, were, in process of time, entered into without their interposition and authority; and in a multiplicity of cases to which the law did not extend. Neither is there any just cause to wonder, that every trifling affront, insult, or injury, which seemed, even in the remotest manner to touch the honour of a gentleman, and particularly of a soldier, would instantaneously rouze his unbridled spirit, and prompt him to draw his sword; and thus to call upon his adversary to make due reparation for the real, or imaginary offence.

A usage, thus commenced, operating upon men of fierce courage, high animal spirits, rude manners, and in that dark period of society, in which the gratification of personal revenge was held, not only venial, but highly honourable, would speedily carry in its train a multiplicity of the most fatal effects.

At an early period of the sixteenth century, a circumstance occurred which gave a tone to the public mind throughout Europe, highly favourable to the adoption and prevalence of this mode of deciding private quarrels. At the breaking up of a treaty between the Emperor Charles V. of Germany and Francis I. of France, the former desired a herald of Francis to acquaint his sovereign, that, in future, he would consider him, not only as a base violator of public faith, but as a stranger to the honour and integrity becoming a gentleman.* Francis

---

* Francis I. was taken prisoner at the battle of Pavia, and Charles V. made proposals to him for the recovery of his liberty, which he rejected with scorn, and pointing a dagger to his breast, exclaimed, " 'Twere better a king

was too high spirited to bear such contumely without the deepest resentment. He had, therefore, recourse to an uncommon expedient to vindicate his sullied honour. Without delay, he sent back the herald, with a cartel of defiance, in which he gave the Emperor " the lie" in due form, challenged him to single combat, requiring him to name the time, and place of the encounter, and the weapons with which he chose to fight. Charles, being in no degree inferior to his rival in spirit or bravery, accepted the challenge; but, after several

should die thus." He became impatient, however, of a personal interview with the Emperor, and at his earnest request, he was at length conveyed to Spain, where Charles then was. After much delay, upon various frivolous pretences, Madrid was fixed on for this important interview; the Emperor, fearing to persist in his unreasonable demands, agreed to relinquish some of his pretensions. Burgundy was, however, to be ceded to him, and the two sons of Francis were to be delivered as hostages for the performance of the articles on the part of the French monarch. As soon, however, as Francis entered his own dominions, he mounted a Turkish horse, and clapping spurs to the animal's sides, he waved his hat several times, exclaiming, " I am a king again!" He refused to fulfil his engagement with Charles, and the Pope absolved him from the oath he had taken at Madrid to give up Burgundy.

messages concerning the arrangement of the circumstances relative to the combat, accompanied with mutual reproaches, bordering on the most indecent scurrility, all thoughts of this duel, which had excited universal attention and interest, were ultimately laid aside.*

The example of two personages, so illustrious, attracted such general notice, and carried with it so much authority, that it possessed considerable influence in introducing an important change in the public mind throughout Europe. In France, the folly, or rather madness of this usage raged

---

* It may be remarked upon the whole of this case, that Francis had written a protest before he signed the treaty, and took the oath to observe it, that any papers he might be compelled to subscribe from necessitous circumstances, should be accounted by him as invalid. Accordingly, when he assembled the States of Burgundy, he was prepared to profit by their objections to that part of the treaty which concerned themselves; and he replied to the Imperial ambassadors, "That, as far as concerned himself, he was willing to fulfil the treaty, but in those matters which affected the French monarchy, he must be guided by the sense of the nation." This answer gave rise to the *holy league* formed against Charles V. by France, England, Venice, Switzerland, Florence, the Pope, and the Milanese.

for ages with such pestilent fury, that the flower of the French noblesse perished by it. Some of the best blood in Christendom was shed, and at particular periods, war itself was scarcely more destructive than these contests of honour. In the time of Henry IV. above 4000 gentlemen perished by duels. It was highly creditable to the reign of Louis XIV. that he exerted all his authority for restraining the madness of this practice; and the severe edicts which he issued against duellists, in a great measure checked its destructive tendency.

It appears, then, that this species of duel, this mode of deciding personal quarrels, has, at no time, rested its foundation in positive law; but that, grafting itself on a vitiated stock, it has, by connivance, become a species of law, possessed of an undefined power and operation, opening an extensive field for the gratification of a variety of bad passions; and by the culpable inactivity of modern legislators, still allowed to remain, as the disgrace of modern times; and an irrefragable proof of the position with which this work commenced, viz. that men, and communities of men, present, in their private and public relations, the extremes of opposite qualities, that is, the most exalted intelligence, and the most ridiculous folly; the most extended and enlightened regard to the public good, and the obstinate retention of the most absurd and injurious usages. For the present age is, doubtless, chargeable with this folly and this absurdity, as long as two private individuals are permitted, in the face of a positive law, enacted against murder, to take this awful law into their own hands, and deliberately, for the purpose of adjusting a private difference, often of the most ridiculous complexion, to fix upon time, place, and seconds, for the purpose of exposing their mutual lives to the chance of palpable destruction.

It is by no means here advanced, that this mode of deciding private quarrels is sanctioned by the law of the land. On the contrary, it is admitted, (on the authority of Coke in his 'Institutes'), "that single combat between any of the King's subjects is strictly prohibited by the laws of this realm." And on this principle, " that in states governed by law, no man, in consequence of any injury whatever, ought to indulge the principle of private revenge;" for revenge, he declares, belongs to the magistrate, who is God's lieutenant. " That it is, also, against the express law of nature, and of nations, for a man to be, ' judex in propria persona,' judge in his own cause," especially, " in duello," in a " single combat," in which, " fury, malice, and revenge, may unfortunately govern and control the judgment."

This acknowledged, and profound sage in British law, proceeds to lay down various maxims of English jurisprudence on this important subject.

1. " That the honour and estimation of individuals, in a personal dispute, may be more justly revenged and repaired by the magistrate in public, than by themselves in private."

2. " That there is nothing honourable which is contradictory to the law of our country, or to the acknowledged laws of nature and of nations."

3. " That whatever is against the laws of God, is impious and dishonourable."

4. " That the imminent danger of the

parties seeking private revenge, proves its folly and evil tendency."

5. " That it is impiously hostile to the origin and nature of man, and to the laws of God, as man is said to be made after the image of God, " Quicunque igitur, effuderit humanum sanguinem, fundetur sanguis illius, ad imaginem quippe Dei factus est homo." " Whoso sheddeth man's blood, by man shall his blood be shed, as in the image of God made he man." " Solus Deus, qui vitam dat, vitæ est Dominus; nec potest quisquam eam justè auferre nisi Deus, vel gerens auctoritatem Dei, ut Judex." " God, who gives life, is the sole lord of life, nor can any justly take it away except God, or a person possessing his authority, as a judge."

In pursuing this usage through the cases in which death does not ensue, the great and profound jurist, already named, proceeds to observe, that even in those cases, in which no fatal effect takes place, and in which no blood is drawn, yet that the very combat for revenge is considered by the English law in the light of an affray, a breach of the King's peace, an affright and terror to the King's subjects, and is punishable by fine and imprisonment, and the finding of sureties for good behaviour, as it is " vi et armis, et contra pacem Domini Regis," &c. " By force and arms an invasion of the peace of our Lord the King," &c. as it is, also, an encroachment upon royal authority for the purpose of revenge, and therefore " contra coronam, et dignitatem," " a disparagement of his crown and dignity." It is, also, an offence, and punishable by law, even previous to combat, by word, writing, or message, to challenge another, as this offence is considered to be " contra pacem, coronam, et dignitatem."

When by single combat an affray is made, any by-stander, though not an officer, may endeavour to separate them, and prevent further danger, and the law gives them encouragement for this purpose; for, if they receive harm by the " affrayeurs," they may have their remedy by law against them; and, if the " affrayeurs" receive hurt by such interference, the stander-by may justify the same, and the " affrayeurs" will have no remedy at law. But if either of the parties be slain or wounded, or so stricken, that he falleth down apparently dead, in that case it is the duty of the standers-by, to apprehend the party so slaying, wounding, or striking; or, to do their utmost to effect this by " hue and cry," or else, for the escape of the offenders, they shall be fined and imprisoned. And if any be commanded to assist, and refuse, or neglect the same, it is considered as a contempt in them, and is punishable by fine and imprisonment.

It has been asserted by very high authority, that the strongest prohibitions and penalties of the law will never be entirely effectual in eradicating this unhappy custom, till a method can be devised of compelling the aggressor to make some other satisfaction to the insulted, or offended party, which the world shall esteem equally reputable as that, which is now given at the hazard of life and fortune, as well of the person insulted, as of him who gives the insult.

To this purpose, Dr. Robertson, in adverting to the celebrated challenge which passed between the Emperor Charles V. and Francis, has observed, " that the dominion of fashion is so powerful, that neither the tyranny of penal laws, nor reverence for religion, has been able entirely to abolish a practice, unknown among the ancients, and not justifiable by any principle of reason; though, at the same time, it must be admitted, that to this absurd custom we must ascribe, in some degree, the extraordinary gentleness and complacency of modern manners, and that respectful attention of one man to another, which, at present, renders the social intercourses of life far more agreeable and decent, than among the most civilized nations of antiquity."

It has, also, been advanced, that public opinion is not easily controlled by civil institutions; for which reason, it may be questioned, whether any regulations can be contrived, of sufficient force, to suppress or change the rule which stigmatizes all scruples about duelling with the reproach of cowardice. The inadequate redress which the law of the land affords for those injuries, which chiefly affect a man in his sensibilities and reputation, by the trifling damages which are recovered, serve only to make the sufferer more ridiculous. The desideratum, then, both in a political and moral view, is:

The discovery of *that principle*, which shall secure the *good order of society*, and especially *military society*, so effectually, as to *suppress* the *spirit* of the *insolent* and the *brutish*, without the *infraction* of *divine* and *human laws;* and, at the same time, to afford *ample redress* to the *injured*.

To the Author of this Work *one principle* appears fully adequate to the removal of the enormous evils connected with the usage in question. But no *soldier* dare enlarge on this principle, or give a *hint* respecting it, in the *discussion* of so *nice* a *question;* a *young soldier*, especially, must for ever *close his lips* upon this *test* of military spirit; for, even a *whisper* on the *Christian doctrine* of "*forbearance* and *forgiveness* of *injuries*," would for ever seal his *doom* as a *military man*.

The *Military Council*, in Ensign Cowell's case, has taught the young soldier a more *powerful*, a more *orthodox doctrine*, than the most dominant *article* of the *Christian canons*. It has taught him, that he must *pursue, even unto blood*, the man who *offends* him; that he must break the most awful *laws of God and man,* in the defence of *personal honour,* and violate even the British " *Articles of War,"* in his onward course of *military spirit.* It matters not whether, in his correct compliance with this great military doctrine, he encounters the *criminal laws* of his *country,* for his line of conduct is *imperatively marked out.* It imports not, whether a *jury* of his *country* find him guilty of " *murder,"* for this infraction of their *common institutes,* he must abide by the *severity of his situation.* If, in this *anomalous condition* of a human being, he receives even the *pardon* of his *Prince,* he must be content, also, to undergo the most *poignant reprehension* from his *military Commander,* for conduct which, if fairly represented, the breath of the *foulest-mouthed obloquy* could not malign him!! If this be a fair statement of the situation of a *British soldier,* of a *British officer,* and that it is, I defy any man to deny, who is a competent judge; what is the *just,* what is the *palpable* inference?

But I must check my *feelings* on this part of the subject, or they may carry me too far.

In stating the existence of an evil in the *bosom* of my native and beloved country, I have traced in its *origin* and in its *history*, that usage which, in a certain degree, *lowers* the *pride* of *our legislation*, degrades the *intellectual* and *moral character* of the *British people*, and, if allowed its *accustomed*, and probably *increasing operation*, on the *higher* and *more polished classes* of the *community*, will continue to depreciate our far-famed system of jurisprudence in the estimation of the *enlightened* and the *good*, to the latest ages of posterity.

But what is the REMEDY for this glaring evil? In the opinion of the Author, few individuals, whatever may be their *intellectual powers*, whatever their *moral wisdom* and *practical experience* of *human institutes*, are competent to the task. It would be presumptuous then in him to obtrude upon his readers all the plans which have suggested themselves to his reflection.

But is *no remedy* to be *attempted?* Is a " *gothic appeal* to *cold iron* " still to *disgrace* the *practice* of *Britons*, and particularly to cast a stigma on that most important part of the community to which it is almost exclusively confined? No; for Englishmen have a paramount claim on the *wisdom*, the *experience*, and the *activity* of their *representatives*, in regard to this awful subject. Let it not, then, be regarded as beneath the occupation of *Parliament*, to add to the multiplicity of benevolent plans which their predecessors have already achieved, some remedy which may tend to annihilate that *most painful, immoral*, and *barbarous* usage, which has originated in superstitious feeling; an usage, which causes the *philosopher* and the *historian* to blush for *human nature*, when recording, even in the darkest ages, the fatal prevalence of so *injurious* and so *silly* a remnant of *gothic ignorance*.

If this Work should fall into the hands, and should stimulate the benevolent genius and exertions of some distinguished individual in *Parliament*; if it should lead him to call in the aid of the most enlightened part of the community to provide an adequate remedy, the Writer would have abundant cause to rejoice, that he has contributed to check an absurd usage, which has compelled many of his high-minded *coun-*

trymen to suffer, in early life, multiplied evils from its pernicious existence. And till the strong arm of *British legislation*, seconded by the undeviating energy of *judicial forms*, shall annihilate this *disgraceful emanation* of *gothic barbarity*, every British officer, and every English gentleman is exposed to similar evils. Till this period takes place, this savage usage must have its full force; for, in *honourable minds*, there is no *alternative* between *death* and *infamy*.

The Author, therefore, purposes to satisfy himself, for the present, with giving a brief outline of a few *calculations*, which occupied his attention when he had completed the following collection.

It appears, that in *one hundred and seventy-two combats* (including *three hundred and forty-four individuals,*) *sixty-nine persons* were *killed;* that in *three* of these *neither* of the *combatants survived;* that *ninety-six* were *wounded, forty-eight* of them *desperately*, and *forty-eight slightly;* that *one hundred* and *eighty-eight* escaped *unhurt*.

From this statement it will be seen that rather *more* than *one*-fifth of the combatants *lost their lives*, and that nearly *one-half* received the bullets of their antagonists.

" It appears, also, that only *eighteen trials* took place; that *six* of the arraigned were " *acquitted,*" *seven* found guilty of " *manslaughter*," and *three* of *murder;*" that *two* were *executed*, and *eight imprisoned* during different periods.

It appears, also, that this *remorseless usage* has, during the period of our investigation, ingulfed within its putrid vortex the names of noblemen, illustrious *statesmen, orators*, and *warriors*. For, in this list will be found the names of York, Norfolk, Richmond, Shelburne, Macartney, Townsend, Bellamont, Exmouth, Talbot, Lauderdale, Lonsdale, Malden, Camelford, Hompesch, Paget, Castlereagh, Belgrave, Petersham, Pitt, Fox, Sheridan, Canning, Tierney, Burdett, &c. &c. with a long list of other names, which, though of *minor*, are still of *interesting import*. But, Reader! peruse for *thyself* the *blood-stained page*; and draw from it those reflections which become thee, as an *English politician*, a *moralist*, and a *man!*

A CHRONOLOGICAL REGISTER

OF

THE PRINCIPAL DUELS

WHICH HAVE BEEN FOUGHT SINCE THE COMMENCEMENT
OF THE REIGNS OF

HIS LATE MAJESTY GEORGE THE THIRD,

AND

HIS PRESENT MAJESTY GEORGE THE FOURTH,

UP TO THE PRESENT PERIOD.

CHRONOLOGICAL REGISTER.

1.

Duel between EARL TALBOT *and* JOHN WILKES, *Esq. October* 5, 1762.

THE dispute between these distinguished characters, originated in words used in the Twelfth Number of the political work, called the "North Briton," published on the 21st of August, 1762, and which conveyed reflections injurious to the feelings of Earl Talbot.

Various letters passed between the parties; and the posture of the times rendering them of national importance, this personal contest itself was viewed with no ordinary degree of interest. The three following letters are selected, as being most appropriate to the object of this Work.

To Colonel Berkeley, (*afterwards* Lord Bottetourt.)

Sir, *Winchester, Sept.* 30, 1762

Lord Talbot, by your message, has at last brought this most important question to the precise point where my first answer to his Lordship fixed it, if he preferred that. As you have only seen the two last letters, I must entreat you to cast your eye over those preceding, because I apprehend they will justify an observation or two I made this morning, when I had the honour of paying my compliments to you at camp. Be assured, that if I am between heaven and earth, I will be on Tuesday evening at Tilbury's, the Red Lion, at Bagshot, and on Wednesday morning will play this duet with his Lordship.

It is a real satisfaction to me, that his Lordship is to be accompanied by a gentleman of Colonel Berkeley's worth and honour.

This will be delivered to you by my adjutant, who attends me to Bagshot. I shall not bring any servant with me, from the fear of any of the parties being known. My pistols only, or his Lordship's, at his option, shall decide this point.

I beg the favour of you to return me the letters, as I mean to leave Winchester this evening. I have Lord Bruce's leave of absence for ten days.

I am, with sincere regard, Sir,
your very humble Servant,
JOHN WILKES.

I hope we may make a "partie quarrée" for supper on Tuesday at Bagshot.

SIR, *Camp near Winchester, Sept. 30, 1762.*
I HAVE read all the letters, and shall depend upon the pleasure of supping with you at Tilbury's, the Red Lion at Bagshot, Tuesday evening. My servant will attend me, as the going alone would give room for suspicion, but you may depend upon his following your direction at Bagshot, and that he shall not be seen where you would not have him. I am much obliged by your favourable opinion, and am,

your very humble Servant,
N. BERKELEY.

To Colonel Wilkes.

To Earl Temple.

Red Lion, at Bagshot,
My Lord,   *Tuesday,* 10 *at Night, Oct.* 5, 1762.

I HAD the honour of transmitting to your Lordship copies of seven letters, which passed between Lord Talbot and me. As the affair is now over, I inclose an original letter of Colonel Berkeley's, with a copy of mine previous to it, which fixed the particulars of our meeting, and therefore remained a secret, very sacredly kept by the four persons concerned.

I came here at three this afternoon, and about five I was told that Lord Talbot and Colonel Berkeley were in the house. Lord Talbot had been here at one, and was gone again, leaving a message, however, that he would soon return. I had continued in the room where I was at my first coming, for fear of raising any suspicion. I sent a compliment to Colonel Berkeley, and that I wished to see him; he was so obliging as to come to me directly. I told him that I supposed we were to sup together with Lord Talbot, whom I was ready to attend

as became a private gentleman; and that
he and Mr. Harris, (Mr. Wilkes's adjutant,)
as our seconds, would settle the business of
the next morning, according to my letter
to him from Winchester, and his answer.
Berkeley said, that his Lordship desired to
finish the business immediately. I replied,
that the appointment was, to sup together
that evening, and to fight in the morning;
that, in consequence of such an arrangement, I had, like an idle man of pleasure,
put off some business of real importance,
which I meant to settle before I went to
bed. I added, that I was come from Med-
nenham Abbey, where the jovial monks of
St. Francis had kept me up till four in the
morning; that the world would therefore
conclude that I was drunk, and form no
favourable opinion of his Lordship from a
duel at such a time; that it more became
us both to take a cool hour of the next
morning, and as early a one as was agreeable to his Lordship. Berkeley said, that
he had undertaken to bring us together,
and as we were both now at Bagshot, he
would leave us to settle our own business.
He then asked me if I would go with him

to his Lordship. I said, I would any moment he pleased. We went directly, with my adjutant.

I found his lordship in an agony of passion. He said, that I had injured him; that he was not used to be injured or insulted. What did I mean? Did I, or did I not, write the North Briton of August 21st, which affronted his honour? He would know: he insisted on a direct answer: here were his pistols. I replied, that he would soon use them; that I desired to know by what right his Lordship catechised me about a paper which did not bear my name: that I should never resolve the question to him, till he made out the right of putting it; and that if I could have entertained any other idea, I was too well bred to have given his Lordship and Colonel Berkeley the trouble of coming to Bagshot. I observed, that I was a private English gentleman, perfectly free and independent, which I held to be a character of the highest dignity: that I obeyed with pleasure a gracious sovereign, but would never submit to the arbitrary dictates of a fellow subject, a Lord Steward of his household; my superior indeed in rank, fortune, and abilities, but my equal only in honour, courage, and liberty. His Lordship then asked me if I would fight him that evening. I said, that I preferred the next morning, as it had been settled before, and gave my reasons. His Lordship replied, that he insisted on finishing the affair immediately. I told him, that I should very soon be ready; that I did not mean to quit him, but would absolutely first settle some important business relative to the education of an only daughter, whom I tenderly loved: that it would take up but very little time, and I would immediately decide the affair in any way he chose, for I had brought both sword and pistols. I rung the bell for pen, ink and paper, desiring his Lordship to conceal his pistols, that they might not be seen by the waiter. He soon after became half frantic, and made use of a thousand indecent expressions, that I should be *hanged, damned,* &c. &c. I said, that I was not to be frightened, nor, in the least, affected by such violence: that God had given me a firmness and spirit, equal to his Lordship's, or any man's: that **cool courage** should always mark me, and that it would be seen how well bottomed he was.

After the waiter had brought pen, ink, and paper, I proposed that the door of the room might be locked, and not opened till our business was decided. His Lordship, on this proposition, became quite outrageous; declared, that this was mere *butchery*, and that I was a wretch, who sought his life. I reminded him that I came there on a point of honour, to give his Lordship satisfaction; that I mentioned the circumstance of locking the door, only to prevent all possibility of interruption; and that I would in every circumstance be governed, not by the turbulence of the most violent temper I had ever seen, but by the calm determinations of our two seconds, to whom I implicitly submitted. His Lordship then asked me if I would deny the paper. I answered, that I would neither own, nor deny it; if I survived, I would afterwards declare, not before.

Soon after, he grew a little cooler, and in a soothing tone of voice, said, I have never, I believe, offended Mr. Wilkes; why has he attacked me? He must be sorry to see me unhappy. I asked, upon what ground his Lordship imputed the paper to me? that Mr. Wilkes would justify any paper to which he had put his name, and would equally assert the privilege of not giving any answer whatever about a paper which he had not: that this was my undoubted right, which I was ready to seal with my blood. He then said, he admired me exceedingly, really loved me, but I was an unaccountable animal — such parts! but would I kill him who had never offended me? &c. &c. &c. We had after this a good deal of conversation about the Bucks Militia, and the day his Lordship came to see us on Wycombe Heath, before I was *Colonel*. He soon after flamed out again, and said to me, You are a murderer, you want to kill me; but I am sure I shall kill you, I know I shall, by G—d! If you will fight, if you will kill me, I hope you will be *hanged;* I know you will. I asked, if I was first to be *killed,* and afterwards to be *hanged?* That I knew his Lordship fought me with the King's pardon in his pocket, and I fought him with a halter about my neck: that I would fight him for all that, and if he fell, I should not tarry here a moment for the tender mercies of such a ministry, but would directly proceed to the next stage, where my valet waited for me, and from thence I would make the best of my way to France, as men of honour were sure of protection in that country. He then told me, that I was an unbeliever, and wished to be killed. I could not help smiling at this, and observed, that we did not meet at Bagshot to settle articles of faith, but points of honour; that indeed I had no fear of dying, but I enjoyed life as much as any man in it; that I was as little subject to be gloomy, or even peevish, as any Englishman whatever; that I valued life, and the fair enjoyments of it so much, I would never quit it by my own consent, except on a call of honour.

I then wrote a letter to your Lordship, respecting the education of Miss Wilkes, and gave you my poor thanks for the steady friendship with which you have so many years honoured me. Colonel Berkeley took the care of the letter, and I have since desired him to send it to Stowe, for the sentiments of the heart at such a moment are beyond all politics, and indeed every thing else, except such virtue as Lord Temple's.

When I had sealed my letter, I told his Lordship I was entirely at his service, and I again desired that we might decide the affair in the room, because there could not be a possibility of interruption; but he was quite inexorable. He then asked me how many times we should fire? I said, that I left it to his choice : I had brought a flask of powder, and a bag of bullets. Our seconds then charged the pistols, which my adjutant had brought; they were large horse-pistols. It was agreed that we should fire at the word of command, to be given by one of our seconds. They tossed up, and it fell to my adjutant to give the word. We then left the inn, and walked to a garden at some distance from the house. It was near seven, and the moon shone bright. We stood about eight yards distant, and agreed not to turn round before we fired, but to continue facing each other. Harris gave the word. Both our fires were in very exact time, but neither took effect. I walked up immediately to his Lordship, and told him that now I avowed the paper. His Lordship paid me the highest encomiums on my courage, and said he would declare every where that I was the noblest fellow God had ever made. He then desired that we might now be good friends, and retire to the inn to drink a bottle of claret together, which we did with great good humour and much laugh.

His Lordship afterwards went to Windsor, Colonel Berkeley and my adjutant to Winchester, and I continue here till to-morrow morning, waiting the return of my valet, to whom I have sent a messenger. Berkeley told me he was grieved for his Lordship's passion, and admired my courage and coolness beyond his farthest idea: that was his expression.

I have a million of other particulars to relate, but I blush already at the length of this letter. Your Lordship will soon see Colonel Berkeley, and I hope in a few days to pay my devoirs at Stowe. I intend to be at Aylesbury Quarter Sessions by Thursday's dinner. My most respectful compliments always attend Lady Temple.

I am ever, my dear Lord, &c. &c.

JOHN WILKES.

Duel between Mr. WILKES *and* Mr. MARTIN, *November*, 1763.

WHEN Mr. Wilkes returned from the House of Commons on Wednesday morning, the 16th of November (the House having sate till that time,) he sent the following letter to Mr. Samuel Martin, late Secretary to the Treasury, who had grossly, but obliquely, insulted him the preceding evening.

SIR,   *Great George-street, Nov.* 16, 1763.

You complained yesterday before five hundred gentlemen, that you had been *stabbed in the dark* by the North Briton. But I believe you were not so much in *the dark,* as you affected, and chose to be. Was the complaint made before so many gentlemen on purpose that they might interpose? To cut off every pretence of this kind, as to the author, I whisper in your ear, that every passage of the North Briton in which you have been named, or alluded to, was written by

your humble Servant,

JOHN WILKES.

To this letter Mr. Martin returned the following answer.

Sir, *Abingdon-street, Nov.* 16, 1763.
As I said in the House of Commons yesterday, that the writer of the North Briton, who had stabbed me in the dark, was a cowardly, as well as a malignant scoundrel, and your letter, of this morning's date, acknowledges that every passage of the North Briton in which I have been named, or even alluded to, was written by yourself; I must take the liberty to repeat, that you are a malignant and infamous scoundrel, and that I desire to give you an opportunity of shewing me, whether the epithet of *cowardly*, was rightly applied or not.

I desire that you may meet me in Hyde Park immediately, with a brace of pistols each, to determine our difference. I shall go to the Ring in Hyde Park, with my pistols so concealed, that no body may see them; and I will wait in expectation of you one hour. As I shall call in my way at your house, to deliver this letter, I propose to go from thence directly to the Ring in Hyde Park; from whence we may proceed, if it be necessary, to any more private place. And I mention, that I shall wait an hour, in order to give you the full time to meet me.

I am, Sir,
your humble Servant,
SAMUEL MARTIN.

The following were the circumstances of the duel.

When the gentlemen met in Hyde Park, they walked together a little while, to avoid some company which seemed coming up to them. They brought each a pair of pistols. When they were alone, the first fire was from Mr. Martin's pistol, which missed Mr. Wilkes; the pistol in Mr. Wilkes's hand only flashed in the pan. The gentlemen then each took one of the remaining pistols: Mr. Wilkes missed; and the ball of Mr. Martin's pistol lodged in Mr. Wilkes's belly. He bled immediately very much. Mr. Martin came up, and desired to give him all the assistance in his power. Mr. Wilkes replied, that Mr. Martin had behaved like a man of honour; that he was killed; and insisted on Mr. Martin's making his immediate escape, adding, that no person should know from him (Mr. Wilkes) how the affair happened. Upon this they parted. Mr. Wilkes was carried home; but would not tell any circumstance of the case, till he found it was perfectly known. He only said to the surgeon, that it was an affair of honour.

The day following, Mr. Wilkes imagining himself in the greatest danger, returned to Mr. Martin his letter, that no evidence might appear against him; and insisted upon it with his own relations, that, in case of his death, no trouble should be given to Mr. Martin, for he had behaved as a man of honour.

Mr. Wilkes was carried home in a chair. Dr. Brocklesby and Mr. Graves (surgeon) were immediately sent for. Mr. Graves extracted the ball, which first struck Mr. Wilkes's coat button, entered his belly about half an inch below the navel, and sunk obliquely, on the right side, towards the groin, but did not penetrate the abdomen. It was extracted behind.

When he was able to write, he sent notice, by letter, to the Speaker of the House of Commons of the condition of his health. On Friday, the 16th of December, the House of Commons made the following order: " That Dr. Heberden, physician, and Mr. Cæsar Hawkins, one of his Majesty's sergeant surgeons, be desired to attend John Wilkes, Esq. from time to time, at proper intervals, to observe the progress of his cure; and that they, together with Dr. Brocklesby and Mr. Graves, do attend this House, to report their opinion thereupon, on the 19th of January next, in case the said John Wilkes, Esq. be not then able to attend in his place."

This Order being sent to Dr. Heberden, by order of the Speaker, he sent it to Dr. Brocklesby, with a letter, desiring to know when he might attend Dr. Brocklesby to Mr. Wilkes. Dr. Brocklesby sent the Order of the House, and Dr. Heberden's letter, to Mr. Wilkes, and requested him to appoint a time when they might wait on him. Mr. Wilkes sent a polite card to Dr. Heberden, saying, that he was so well satisfied with the attention and skill of Dr. Brocklesby and Mr. Graves, that he did not wish

G

to see Dr. Heberden for some weeks. He sent a similar card to Mr. Hawkins.

Mr. Martin immediately proceeded to Paris; and on Mr. Wilkes's arrival in that city, notes, and a friendly visit, were exchanged between them.

3.

Duel between Mr. PLEDGER *and a Naval Officer, May* 20, 1763.

A duel was fought near Lambeth Marsh between Mr. Pledger and an Officer in the navy, occasioned by the late party disputes. Mr. Pledger was shot through the arm, and the bone was shattered. The ball went through the officer's wig, but did him no harm. They shook hands, and the Officer waited upon the wounded man home.

4.

Duel between Cornet GARDINER *and the Rev. Mr.* HILL, *February* 8, 1764.

A duel was fought between Cornet Gardener, of the Carabineers, and the Rev.

Mr. Hill, Chaplain of Bland's Dragoons, when the latter received a wound, of which he died two days after.

The duel took place on Epping Forest.

The Coroner's Jury, after sitting twelve hours on the body, brought in their verdict, " Manslaughter at large."

Hill was an Irish gentleman, of good address, great sprightliness, and possessed an excellent talent of preaching: but was of rather too volatile a turn for his profession.

5.

An authentic Narrative of the Duel between LORD BYRON *and* W. CHAWORTH, *Esq.*

LORD Byron and Mr. Chaworth were neighbours in the country; and it was their custom to meet, with other gentlemen of Nottinghamshire, at the Star and Garter Tavern in Pall-Mall, at what was called the Nottinghamshire Club.

The meeting at which the unlucky dispute arose, that produced the duel, was on the 26th of January, 1765, and at which were present: John Hewett, Esq. who sate as Chairman, Lord Byron, the Honourable Thomas Willoughby, Sir Robert Burdett, Frederick Montagu, John Sherwin, Francis Molyneux, William Chaworth, George Donston, and Charles Mellish, jun. Esquires.

Their usual hour of dining was soon after four, and the rule of the Club was, to have a bill and a bottle brought in at seven o'clock.

Till this hour all was jollity and good humour. But Mr. Hewett, who was toastmaster, happening to start some conversation about the best method of preserving the game, setting the laws in being for that purpose out of the question, the subject was taken up by Mr. Chaworth and Lord Byron, who happened to be of different opinions, Mr. Chaworth insisting on severity against poachers and unqualified persons, and Lord Byron declaring, that the way to have most game, was, to take no care of it at all. Mr. Hewett's opinion was, that the most effectual way would be, to make the game the property of the owner of the soil. The debate became general, but was carried on with acrimony only between Lord Byron and Mr. Chaworth; the latter, in confirmation of what he had said, insisting, that Sir Charles Sedley and himself had more game on five acres, than Lord Byron had on all his manors. Lord Byron, in answer to this, proposed a bet of a hundred guineas, and Mr. Chaworth called for pen, ink, and paper, to reduce the wager to writing, in order to take it up; but Mr. Sherwin, treating it in a jesting manner, as a bet that never could be decided, no bet was laid, and the conversation went on.

Mr. Chaworth said, " that were it not for Sir Charles Sedley's care and his own, Lord Byron would not have a hare on his estate." And Lord Byron asking, with a smile, " What Sir Charles Sedley's manors were?" was answered by Mr. Chaworth, Nuttal and Bulwell. Lord Byron did not dispute Nuttal, but added, that Bulwell was his own. On which Mr. Chaworth, with some heat, replied, " If you want information with respect to Sir Charles Sedley's manors, he lives at Mr. Cooper's, in Dean-street, and I doubt not will be ready to give you satisfaction; and as to myself, your Lordship knows where to find me in Berkeley-row," or words to that effect.

These words, uttered in a particular manner, could admit of no reply; and, at once, put an end to the subject of discourse. Every gentleman in the company fell into chat with him who sate next to him; and nothing more was said, generally, till Mr. Chaworth called to settle the reckoning, as was his general practice; in doing which, Mr. Fynmore, the master of the tavern, observed him a little flurried; for, in marking, he made a small mistake. The book had lines ruled in checks, and against each member present, a cypher was placed; but, if absent, 5*s.* was set down. He placed 5*s.* against Lord Byron's name; but Mr. Fynmore observing to him that his Lordship was present, he corrected his mistake.

In a few minutes after this, Mr. Chaworth having paid his reckoning, went out, and was followed by Mr. Donston, who entered into discourse with him at the head of the stairs, and Mr. Chaworth asked him particularly, if he had attended to the conversation between himself and Lord Byron, and if he thought he had been short in what he had said on the subject? To which Mr. Donston said, "No; he had gone rather too far upon so trifling an occasion, but did not believe that Lord Byron or the company would think any more about it; and after a little ordinary discourse had passed, they parted. Mr. Donston returned to the company, and Mr. Chaworth turned to go down stairs: but just as Mr. Donston entered the door, he met Lord Byron coming out, and they passed, as there was a large screen that covered the door, without knowing each other. Lord Byron found Mr. Chaworth still on the stairs, and it now remains a doubt, whether Lord Byron called upon Mr. Chaworth, or Mr. Chaworth upon Lord Byron; but both went to the first landing-place, having dined upon the second floor, and both called the waiter to shew an empty room, which a waiter did, and having first opened the door himself, and placed a small tallow candle, which he had in his hand, on the table, he retired; when the gentlemen entered, and pulled the door after them.

In a few minutes, the affair was decided; the bell was rung, but by whom is uncertain; the waiter went up, and perceiving what had happened, ran down stairs frightened, told his master the catastrophe, who ran instantly up stairs, and found the two combatants standing close together. Mr. Chaworth had his sword in his left hand, and Lord Byron his in his right. Lord Byron's left hand was round Mr. Chaworth, as Mr. Chaworth's right hand was round Lord Byron's neck and over his shoulders, He desired Mr. Fynmore to take his sword, and Lord Byron delivered up his at the same time. One, or both, called to him to get some help immediately, and in a few minutes Mr. Hawkins, the surgeon, was sent for, who came accordingly.

In the mean time, Mr. Montague, Mr. Hewett, Mr. Donston, Mr. Willoughby, Mr. Molyneux, and Mr. Sherwin, had entered the room.

The account Mr. Chaworth then gave was, " that he could not live many hours; that he forgave Lord Byron, and hoped the world would; that the affair had passed in the dark, only a small tallow candle burning in the room; that Lord Byron asked him if he meant the conversation on the game to Sir Charles Sedley or him? To which he replied, If you have any thing to say, we had better shut the door; that while he was doing this, Lord Byron bid him draw, and in turning, he saw his Lordship's sword half drawn; on which he whipped out his own, and made the first pass; the sword being through his Lordship's waistcoat, he thought he had killed him, and asking whether he was not mortally wounded, Lord Byron, while he was speaking, shortened his sword, and stabbed him in the belly."

When Mr. Hawkins, the surgeon, came in, he found Mr. Chaworth sitting by the fire, with the lower part of his waistcoat open, his shirt bloody, and his hand upon his belly. He was very earnest to know if he thought him in imminent danger: and being answered in the affirmative, he desired his uncle, Levinz, might be sent for, that he might settle his private affairs; and in the mean time, gave Mr. Hawkins a particular detail of what had passed. He said, " That Lord Byron and he entered the room together, Lord Byron leading the way; that his Lordship, in walking forwards, said, something relative to the former dispute, on which he proposed fastening the door; that on turning himself round from this act, he perceived his Lordship with his sword either drawn, or nearly so: on which, he instantly drew his own, and made a thrust at him, which he thought had wounded or killed him: that he then perceived his Lordship shorten his sword to return the thrust, and thought to have parried it with his left hand, at which he looked twice, imagining he had cut it in the attempt: that he felt the sword enter his body, and go deep through his back: that he struggled, and being the stronger man, disarmed his Lordship, and expressed a concern, as under an apprehension of having mortally wounded him: that Lord Byron replied, by saying something to the like effect; adding at the same time, 'that he hoped now he would allow him to be as brave a man as any in the kingdom."

Mr. Hawkins adds, that pained and distressed as Mr. Chaworth then was, and under the immediate danger of death, he repeated what he had heard he had declared to his friends before—" That he had rather be in his present situation than live under the misfortune of having killed another person."—After a little while he seemed to grow stronger, and he was then removed to his own house, where Mr. Adair, another surgeon, Mr. Mann, an apothecary, and Dr. Addington, his physician, came to the assistance of Mr. Hawkins, but no relief could be given him. He continued sensible, however, till the time of his death.

Mr. Levinz being now come, Mr. Partington, an attorney, was sent for to make his will, for which he gave very sensible and distinct instructions. And while Mr. Partington was employed in his business, he gave Mr. Levinz, at his request, the same account which he had given before to Mr. Hawkins, lamenting at the same time his own folly, in fighting in the dark, an expression that certainly conveyed no imputation on Lord Byron, and implied no more than this—that by fighting with a dim light, he had given up the advantage of his own superiority in swordmanship, and had been led into the mistake, that he was in the breast of his Lordship, when he was only entangled in his waistcoat. For, under that mistake he certainly was, when Lord Byron shortened his sword, and ran him through the body. He added to Mr. Levinz, that he died as a man of honour, and expressed his satisfaction that he was in his present situation, rather than in that of having the life of any man to answer for.

Mr. Partington, when he had finished the business he was sent for, and the will was properly executed, recollected the probability that he should one day be called upon to give testimony to the dying words of his unhappy client; and accordingly, with the caution that always accompanies a thorough knowledge of the law, he thought proper to commit to writing the last words he was heard to say on this occasion. This writing was put into the hands of Mr. Levinz, and gave rise to a report, that a paper was written by the deceased, and sealed up, not to be opened till the time that Lord Byron should be tried. But no paper whatever was written by Mr. Chaworth; and that written by Mr. Partington was as follows:—

" Sunday morning, the 27th of January, about three o'clock, Mr. Chaworth said—

"That my Lord's sword was half-drawn, and that he, *knowing the man,* immediately, or as quick as he could, whips out his sword, and had the first thrust; that then my Lord wounded him, and he disarmed my Lord, who then said—By G--d, I have as much courage as any man in England."

These are the particulars of this unfortunate affair: by which it should seem, that neither Mr. Chaworth himself, nor any of his friends, could blame Lord Byron for the part he had in his death. Mr. Chaworth, it is manifest, was under the apprehension of having mortally wounded Lord Byron, and Lord Byron, being still engaged, had a right to avail himself of that mistake for the preservation of his own life. His Lordship himself, no doubt, may wish that he had, in that situation, disabled him only; but in the heat of duelling, who can always be collected?

Some time after this unhappy affair, Lord Byron surrendered himself to be tried by his Peers. And on the 16th of April, 1765, about half an hour after nine in the morning, his Lordship, escorted by parties of the Horse and Foot Guards, and attended by the Lieutenant-Governor and Constable of the Tower, and another gentleman, was brought for that purpose in a coach, by the New Road, Southwark, to Westminster Hall; and in the evening, between five and six, his Lordship was conducted back the same way, before all the witnesses for the prosecution could be examined.

The trial being resumed the next day, as soon as their Lordships had examined the rest of the witnesses in support of the charge against Lord Byron, the Solicitor General summed up the evidence. After which, Lord Byron, who declined examining any witnesses on his own behalf, told their Lordships, that what he had to offer in his own vindication, he had committed to writing, and begged that it might be read by the clerk, as he feared his own voice, considering his present situation, would not be heard.

His speech was accordingly read by the clerk in a very audible and distinct manner, and contained an exact detail of all the particulars relating to the melancholy affair between him and Mr. Chaworth. He said, he declined entering into the circumstances of Mr. Chaworth's behaviour any farther than was necessary for his own defence, expressed his deep and unfeigned sorrow for the event, and reposed himself with the utmost confidence, on their Lordship's justice and humanity, and would with cheerfulness acquiesce in the sentence of the noblest and most equitable judicature in the world, whether it were for life or for death.

The Peers then adjourned to their own house, and after some time returned, when they found his Lordship—"Guilty of Manslaughter"—and as by an old statute, Peers are in all cases where Clergy are allowed, to be dismissed without burning in the hand, loss of inheritance, or corruption of blood, his Lordship was immediately dismissed on paying his fees.

The witnesses examined on behalf of the crown were the several gentlemen in company at the Star and Garter Tavern when the accident happened, the Master and Waiters, Mr. Hawkins and Mr. Adair, the Surgeons who attended Mr. Chaworth, his Uncle, and the Lawyer who made his will.

The Counsel for his Lordship were the Honourable Mr. Charles Yorke, and Alexander Wedderburn, Esq.; Attorney, Mr. Potts.—Against his Lordship, the Attorney General, the Solicitor General, Mr. Sergeant Glyn, Mr. Stowe, Mr. Cornwall: Attorney, Mr. Joynes.

6.

Duel between LORD KILMAURS *and a French Officer.   Marseilles, May,* 1765.

LORD Kilmaurs, the Earl of Glencairn's eldest son, is one of the best natured persons in the world, but has the misfortune to be rather deaf: and being one evening at the play, he talked rather loud to the person who sat next to him, as people under his misfortune generally do. This happened to offend a French Officer in the same box, who said to his Lordship " Paix," which is as much as to say in English, " Pray be quiet," which word the officer repeated two or three times without the other's hearing it. Upon which, the officer, with a fierce look, said aloud "Taisez vous," which word implies the most insolent reprimand. His

Lordship heard this, and saw the supercilious air that accompanied it, and made as sharp a reply as it deserved —" That as the other had no right to command silence there, he should shew his contempt of his insolence by talking still louder"—which he accordingly did. The officer soon after left the box, and as his Lordship's ill stars would have it, he left that box also, and went into another, where the same officer was, without the least thought of what had passed. Looking about him on entering the box, he cast his eyes on the officer without recollecting him. The Frenchman, fired with resentment, ran up close, to him, and said " What do you mean by staring at me ?" The other answered—" He thought he might look at any body." To which the Frenchman, in a rage, said, " He was not to be so treated with impunity," and without another word, except " Come along," he pulled his Lordship by the arm out of the box, and in the middle of the street, struck him across the shoulder with his naked sword. Upon which, his Lordship drew and made a pass or two, and before any one arrived to part them, received the sword of his antagonist in the pit of his stomach, and it passed through his right shoulder; on which they were parted. They were immediately surrounded by numberless spectators. At first his Lordship was hardly sensible of his wound; but in a few moments, he dropped down speechless, in which situation he must inevitably have been smothered by the pressing on of the crowd, had not the Duke de Pequigny brought the guards to keep them off. Here again he ran the risk of being stifled with his own blood, had not a surgeon pressed through the crowd, cut his stock and the neck of his shirt, and applied some drops to his nostrils. He remained several hours speechless, with almost every mortal symptom. These, however, passed off: and in three days, he was out of danger. The officer took post immediately into the Pope's dominions at Avignon, and a short detail of the affair was sent to the British Ambassador at Paris, referring it entirely to his Excellency to manage the matter as he thought proper.

7.
Duel between Captain I——, and Major A——. September 22, 1765.

A duel was fought near Kennington Common, between Captain I——, and Major A——, when the latter received a ball in his breast, which came out at his side.

The wounded gentleman was carried home to his house in Oxendon Street, Leicester Fields, when several eminent surgeons were sent for, who declared the wound to be extremely dangerous, though they were not without hopes of ultimate recovery.

Captain I—— made his escape, though closely pursued. Major A—— is about thirty years of age, universally respected, and possesses a plentiful fortune, exclusive of his commission.

8.
Duel between Major H——TH *and Lieutenant* H——. *May* 14, 1766.

A duel was fought at Gosport, between Major H——th of the Marines, and Lieutenant H——, an engineer, in which they were both wounded. The former received a deep wound in one of his thighs, and the latter was slightly wounded in his hand, and one of his thighs.

9.

Duel between Sieur CHELAIS *and Sieur* REGUIN. *October,* 1769.

The Sieur Chelais, Member of Parliament in France, was condemned to be broken upon the wheel for the murder of the Sieur Reguin, captain in the legion of Flanders, by challenging him to fight, covering himself with armour, and when the sword of his antagonist was broken in the attack, most treacherously assassinating him, by stabbing him when he was down. He has, however made his escape for the present; but it is hoped that no State will protect him.

10.

Duel between HENRY FLOOD *and* JAMES AGAR, *Esqrs. October,* 1769.

A duel was fought in Ireland between Henry Flood, and James Agar, Esqrs., in which the latter was shot dead.

An old quarrel had long subsisted between them, which they at length agreed to decide in this manner, and which proved fatal to the first aggressor.

11.

Duel between GEORGE GARRICK, *Esq. and* Mr. BADDELEY. *March* 17, 1770.

A duel was fought in Hyde Park, between George Garrick, Esq., and Mr. Baddeley, both of Drury Lane Theatre, when the former having received the fire of his antagonist, discharged his pistol into the air, which produced a reconciliation.

12.

Duel between LORD MILTON *and* LORD POULETT. *January* 29, 1771.

This morning at 10 o'clock, Lords Milton and Poulett finished their dispute behind Bedford House.

Lord John Cavendish was Lord Milton's second, and Captain Kelly, Lord Poulett's. When they had taken their ground, Lord Milton desired Lord Poulett to fire first, which he did, and the ball entered Lord Milton's belly. This wound prevented farther proceedings.

13.
Duel between Mr. Mc.Lean, *Jun. and Mr.* Cameron. *May* 24, 1772.

Mr. Mc.Lean, Jun. of Gartmoor, in Scotland, being at supper with a select party, at a friend's house, words arose between him and Mr. Cameron, on an old grudge, when the latter gave him the lie, on which a duel ensued, and Mr. Mc.Lean was killed on the spot. His mother on hearing of this melancholy event, was instantly deprived of her senses; and Miss Mc.Leod, a young lady to whom Mr. Mc.Lean was soon to have been married, was seized with fits, and died three days after.

14.
Duel between the Marquis *of* Fleury, *and an Officer of distinction.* *July* 28, 1772.

A duel was fought near Paris between the Marquis of Fleury, son of the Duke of Fleury, and an officer of distinction in the

Regiment of Touraine. The officer was killed, and the Marquis's arm was broken.

15.

Duel between RICHARD BRINSLEY SHERIDAN, *Esq. and Mr.* MATTHEWS.

WHEN Mr. Sheridan became the avowed suitor of Miss Linley, the celebrated vocal performer, her father, the late ingenious composer, was not at first propitious to his passion, and he had many rivals to overcome in his attempts to gain the lady's affections. His perseverance, however, increased with the difficulties that presented themselves, and his courage and resolution in vindicating Miss Linley's reputation from a calumnious report which had been basely thrown out against it, obtained for him the fair prize for which he twice exposed his life.

Mr. Matthews, a gentleman then well known in the fashionable circles at Bath, had caused a paragraph to be inserted in a public paper at that place, which tended to prejudice the character of this young lady, and Mr. Sheridan immediately applied for redress to the printer, who communicated the author's name.

Mr. Matthews had, in the mean time, set out for London, and was closely pursued by Mr. Sheridan. They met, and fought a duel with swords, at a tavern in Henrietta Street, Covent Garden. Mr. Sheridan's second on the occasion, was his brother, Charles Francis, the late Secretary at war in Ireland. Great courage and skill were displayed on both sides; but Mr. Sheridan having succeeded in disarming his adversary, compelled him to sign a formal retraction of the paragraph which had been published.

The conqueror instantly returned to Bath, and thinking, that as the insult had been publicly given, the apology should have equal notoriety, he caused it to be published in the same paper. Mr. Matthews soon heard of this circumstance, and irritated at his defeat, as well as the use which his antagonist had made of his apology, repaired to Bath, determined to call upon Mr. Sheridan for satisfaction. A message was accordingly sent, and a meeting agreed to. Mr. Sheridan would have been justified, according to the most delicate punctilios of honour, in declining the call, but he silenced all the objections that were started by his friends, and the parties met on Kingsdown.

The victory was desperately contested, and after a discharge of pistols, they fought with swords. They were both wounded, and closing with each other, fell on the ground, where the fight was continued, until they were separated. They received several cuts and contusions in this arduous struggle for life and honour, and a part of his opponent's weapon was left in Mr. Sheridan's ear.

Miss Linley did not suffer a long time to elapse before she rewarded Mr. Sheridan for the dangers he had braved in her defence, by accompanying him on a matrimonial excursion to the continent. The ceremony was again performed on their return to England, with the consent of the lady's parents.

16.

Duel between LORD TOWNSEND *and the* EARL *of* BELLAMONT. *February* 2, 1773.

This afternoon, the long subsisting difference between Lord Townsend and the Earl of Bellamont was finally decided, in Mary-le-bone Fields, when the latter received a ball in the right side of his belly, near the groin; the event of which the surgeons cannot decide.

They were armed with small swords, and a case of pistols; but it was agreed to use the latter first. Lord Townsend fired first, which gave the unfortunate wound, and Lord Bellamont discharged his pistol immediately after, without effect. The seconds were the Hon. Mr. Dillon, for Lord Bellamont, and Lord Ligonier for Lord Townsend.

Lord Bellamont was immediately taken up and put into a chaise: but from the agony arising from his wound, he could not bear the motion. A chair was, therefore, immediately sent for, to carry him to his lodging, where, when he arrived, he desired to be laid on his back. Mr. Bromfield and other surgeons were immediately called in, who endeavoured, but in vain, to extract the ball. His lordship ultimately recovered after great suffering.

17.

Duel between Mr. SCAWEN *and Mr.* FITZGERALD. *September* 1, 1773.

THIS day a duel was fought between Mr.

Scawen and Mr. Fitzgerald, near Lisle, in which neither of the gentlemen received any hurt. Mr. Fitzgerald fired two pistols, one by design, and one by accident. Mr. Scawen fired one in the air, when making some slight apology for the cause of the duel, the parties were reconciled, and returned highly satisfied with the issue of the affair.

18.

Duel between Mr. WHATELY *and* JOHN TEMPLE, *Esq. Lieutenant Governor of New Hampshire. December* 11, 1773.

A duel was fought in Hyde Park, between Mr. Whately, brother of Mr. Whately, late Secretary to the Treasury, and John Temple, Esq. Lieutenant Governor of New Hampshire, when the former was dangerously wounded.

The cause of quarrel was—the discovery of the confidential letters written by Messrs. Hutchinson, Oliver, Paxton, &c. &c. which were lately laid before the Assembly at Boston, and have been since published in most of the London papers.

Soon after this duel was fought, the following information was given to the public by Doctor Franklin.

Finding that two gentlemen have been unfortunately engaged in a duel, about a transaction, and its circumstances, of which both of them are totally ignorant and innocent, I think it incumbent on me to declare (for the prevention of farther mischief, as far as such a declaration may contribute to prevent it) that I alone am the person, who obtained, and transmitted, to Boston, the letters in question. Mr. Whately could not communicate them, because they were never in his possession : and, for the same reason, they could not be taken from him by Mr. Temple. They were not of the nature of *private letters between friends.* They were written by public officers to persons in public stations, on public affairs, and intended to produce public measures. They were, therefore, handed to other public persons, who might be influenced by them to produce those measures. Their tendency was to incense the mother-country against her colonies, and, by the steps recommended, to widen the breach, which they effected. The chief caution expressed with regard to privacy was, to keep their contents from the colony agents, who, the writers apprehended, might return them, or copies of them, to America. That apprehension was, it seems, well-founded; for the first agent, who laid his hands on them, thought it his duty to transmit them to his constituents.

(*Signed*) BENJAMIN FRANKLIN.
Agent for the House of Representatives of the Massachussets Bay.

19.

Duel between Captain STONEY *and the Rev. Mr.* BATE. *January* 13, 1777.

A rencontre happened at the Adelphi Tavern in the Strand, between Captain Stoney and Mr. Bate, Editor of the Morning Post.

The cause of quarrel arose from some offensive paragraphs, that had appeared in the "Morning Post," highly reflecting on the character of a lady of rank. After having discharged their pistols at each other without effect, they drew their swords; and Mr. Stoney received a wound in the breast and arm, and Mr. Bate, one in the thigh. Mr. Bate's sword bent, and slanted against the Captain's breast bone, of which Mr. Bate apprising him, Captain Stoney called to him to straighten it; and, in the interim, while the sword was under his foot for that purpose, the door was broke open, or the death of one of the parties would most certainly have ensued. On the Saturday following Captain S. married the lady, whom he had thus defended at the hazard of his own life.

20.

Duel between COUNT RICE *and* VISCOUNT DU BARRY. *Bath, November* 23, 1778.

ON Saturday the 17th instant, Count Rice, and Viscount du Barry, being together in the house of the latter, a question arose between them, about which they disagreed; and in the heat of the dispute, upon an assertion of Count Rice, Viscount du Barry said, " Cela n'est pas vrai," to which Count Rice immediately observed, " You probably do not observe the idea that expression conveys in the language you speak in, and that it admits but of one very disagreeable interpretation." Upon which the other replied, " You may interpret it as you please." This ungentleman-like treatment having provoked the resentment of Count Rice, and Viscount du Barry offering no satisfaction, they immediately sent for seconds, who did not quit them till they got to Claverton Down, where they remained, together with a surgeon, till day-light, when they took the field, each armed with two pistols, and a sword. The ground being marked out by the seconds, the Viscount du Barry fired first, and lodged a ball in Count Rice's thigh, which penetrated as far as the bone. Count Rice fired his pistol, and wounded the Viscount in the breast. He went back two or three steps, then came forward again, and both at the same time presented their pistols to each other. The pistols flashed together in the pan, though one only was discharged. They then threw away their pistols, and took to their swords. When Count Rice had advanced within a few yards of the Viscount, he saw him fall, and heard him cry out, " Je vous demande ma vie."—To which Count Rice answered, " Je vous la donne." But in a few seconds the Viscount fell back, and expired.

Count Rice was brought with difficulty to Bath, being dangerously wounded. But he afterwards recovered.

The Coroner's Inquest sat on the Viscount's body last Saturday; and after a mature examination of the witnesses, and the Viscount's servant, brought in their verdict, " Manslaughter."

21.

Duel between a Lieut.-Colonel, and a Lieutenant of Militia. August 25, 1779.

A duel was fought at Coxheath between a Lieutenant of militia and a Lieut.-Colonel, when the latter was shot in the left breast, and expired immediately. The deceased had charged the Lieutenant with exciting his men to mutiny, of which he was honorably acquitted by a Court Martial.

22.

Duel between the Hon. CHARLES JAMES FOX *and Mr.* ADAM. *November* 30, 1779.

MR. Fox having in debate, one day last week, animadverted, with some degree of asperity, on a particular species of argument, frequently made use of by the friends of Ministers, viz. " That bad as the Ministry were, it was not certain that the nation would be at all bettered by taking their opponents." A Mr. Adam, who had made use of that argument in the same debate, called on Mr. Fox, some days after, for an explanation.

The following letters passed on the above occasion.

St. Alban's Tavern, Saturday, 4 *o'clock, Afternoon.*

MR. ADAM presents his compliments to Mr. Fox, and begs leave to represent to him, that upon considering again and again what had passed between them last night, it is impossible for him to have his character cleared to the public, without inserting

I

the following paragraph in the newspapers: — We have authority to assure the Public, that in a conversation that passed between Mr. Fox and Mr. Adam, in consequence of the debate in the House of Commons on Thursday last, Mr. Fox declared, that how much his speech may have been misrepresented, he did not mean to throw any personal reflection upon Mr. Adam.

Major Humberstone does me the honour of delivering this to you, and will bring your answer.

To the Hon. Charles James Fox.

Sir,

I AM very sorry it is utterly inconsistent with my ideas of propriety, to authorize the putting any thing into the newspapers, relative to a speech which, in my opinion, required no explanation. You, who heard the speech, must know, that it did convey no personal reflection upon you, unless you felt yourself in the predicament upon which I animadverted. The account of my speech in the newspapers is certainly incorrect, and certainly unauthorized by me; and therefore, with respect to them, I have nothing to say.

Neither the conversation that passed at Brookes's, nor this letter, are of a secret nature; and if you have any wish to relate the one, or to shew the other, you are perfectly at liberty so to do.

I am, &c. &c.

Chesterfield Street, ½ *past* 2, *Sunday, Nov.* 28.
To —— *Adam, Esq.*

SIR,

As you must be sensible that the speech, printed in the newspapers, reflects upon me personally; and as it is from them only that the public can have their information, it is evident that, unless that is contradicted by your authority in as public a manner as it was given, my character must be injured. Your refusal to do this entitles me to presume, that you approve of the manner in which that speech has been given to the public, and justifies me in demanding the only satisfaction such an injury will admit of.

Major Humberstone is empowered to settle all particulars; and the sooner this affair is brought to a conclusion, the more agreeable to me.

I have the honour to be, &c. &c.

To the Hon. Charles James Fox.

IN consequence of the above, the parties met, according to agreement, at eight o'clock in the morning. After the ground was measured out, at the distance of fourteen paces, Mr. Adam desired Mr. Fox to fire; to which Mr. Fox replied, " Sir, I have no quarrel with you, do you fire," Mr. Adam then fired, and wounded Mr. Fox, which we believe was not at all perceived by Mr. Adam, as it was not distinctly seen by either of ourselves. Mr. Fox then fired, without effect. We then interfered, asking Mr. Adam if he was satisfied. Mr. Adam replied, " Will Mr. Fox declare he meant no personal attack upon my character?" Upon which Mr. Fox said, this was no place for apology, and desired him to go on. Mr. Adam fired his second pistol without effect. Mr. Fox fired his remaining pistol in the air; and then saying, as the affair was ended, he had no difficulty in declaring, he meant no more personal affront to Mr. Adam than he did to either of the other gentlemen present. Mr. Adam replied, " Sir, you have behaved like a man of honour."

Mr. Fox then mentioned that he believed himself wounded ; and upon his opening his waistcoat, it was found it was so, but to all appearance, slightly. The parties then separated, and Mr. Fox's wound, on examination, was found not likely to produce any dangerous consequences.

Richard Fitzpatrick,—Second to Mr. Fox.
T. Mackenzie Humberstone,—Second to Mr. Adam.

23.

Duel between Counsellor R—— and ——.
November, 1779.

A REMARKABLE trial lately happened in the Court of King's Bench, in Ireland. A Counsellor R—— had fought a duel with a gentleman, and killed him. He traversed the indictment, and imagined the Jury, as usual, would bring in their verdict of " Manslaughter." But the Barrister found himself mistaken. They deemed the intentions of two men going out, premeditatedly, to fight, to be ' Malice aforethought;' and to the astonishment of the Court, brought the prisoner in " Guilty,"—Death. The Judges desired them to recommend him to the Bench, as an object of mercy. They did it with reluctance. This may probably put a stop to the practice of duelling in Ireland.

24.

Duel between the Earl *of* Shelburne *and Colonel* Fullarton. *March* 20, 1780.

Mr. Fullarton, Member for Plympton, and late secretary to Lord Stormont, in his Embassy to the Court of France, complained to the House of the ungentlemanlike behaviour of the Earl of Shelburne, who, he said, with all the aristocratic insolence that marks that nobleman's character, had, in effect, *dared* to say, that he and his regiment were as ready to act against the liberties of England, as against her enemies.

This occasioned some altercation between those who were the friends of each party; but being generally thought unparliamentary, it went at that time no farther.

March 22.

THIS morning, in consequence of the altercation above alluded to, a duel was fought between the Earl of Shelburne and Mr. Fullarton, of which the following is an authentic narrative.

LORD Shelburne, with Lord Frederick Cavendish for his second, and Mr. Fullarton, with Lord Balcarras for his second, met at half past five in Hyde-Park, March 22, 1780. Lord Balcarras and Lord F. Cavendish proposed that both parties should obey the seconds. Lord Shelburne and Mr. Fullarton walked together, while Lord Balcarras and Lord F. Cavendish adjusted all ceremonials; and fixed on pistols as the proper weapons. When they came to the ground, Lord Shelburne told them that his pistols were already loaded, and offered to draw them, which was rejected by Lord Balcarras and Colonel Fullarton; upon which Lord Balcarras loaded Colonel Fullarton's pistols. The seconds having agreed that twelve paces was a proper distance, the parties took their ground. Colonel Fullarton desired Lord Shelburne to fire, which his Lordship declined; and Colonel Fullarton was ordered by the seconds to fire. He fired and missed. Lord Shelburne returned it, and missed. Mr. Fullarton then fired his second pistol, and hit Lord Shelburne in the right groin, which his Lordship signified; upon which every body ran up; the seconds interfered. Lord F. Cavendish offered to take the pistol from Lord Shelburne; but his Lordship refused to deliver it up, saying,—" I have not fired that pistol." Mr. Fullarton returned immediately to his ground, which he had left with a view of assisting his Lordship, and repeatedly desired his Lordship to fire at him. Lord Shelburne said, "Sure, Sir, you do not think I would fire my pistol at you;" and fired it in the air. The parties and their seconds joined together. Lord Balcarras asked Lord Shelburne if he had any difficulty in declaring he meant nothing personal to Colonel Fullarton. His Lordship replied, "You know it has taken another course; this is no time for explanation." His Lordship then said to Colonel Fullarton, "Although I am wounded, I am able to go on if you feel any resentment." Colonel Fullarton said, "He hoped he was incapable of harbouring such a sentiment." Lord F. Cavendish declared, that from the character he had heard of Colonel Fullarton, he believed so. Colonel Fullarton said, "As your Lordship is wounded, and has fired in the air, it is impossible for me to go on."

Lord Balcarras and Lord F. Cavendish immediately declared, "That the parties had ended the affair, by behaving as men of the strictest honour."

On hearing of the above affair, the following message was sent from the City.

"The Committee of Common Council for corresponding with the Committees appointed, or to be appointed, by the several counties, cities, and boroughs, in this kingdom, anxious for the preservation of the valuable life of so true a friend of the people as the Earl of Shelburne, respectfully enquire after his lordship's safety, highly endangerd, in consequence of his upright and spirited conduct in Parliament.

By Order of the Committee,

W. RIX.

The Earl of Shelburne.

25.

Duel between Mr. DONOVAN *and Captain* JAMES HANSON. *April,* 1780.

LAST week, at the assizes at Kingston, in Surrey, the trials on the Crown side came on before the Hon. Mr. Justice Gould, and a special jury, when Mr. Donovan (who voluntarily surrendered himself) was tried for having killed, in a duel, Captain James Hanson. It appeared by a number of respectable witnesses, that the deceased was entirely in fault, and had forced Mr. Donovan to meet him in a field near the Dog and Duck. It also appeared that the only ground of quarrel between the prisoner and the deceased was, that Mr. Donovan interfered between Captain Hanson and another person, and prevented their fighting; on which Captain Hanson gave him very abusive language, and insisted that " he would make him smell powder."

The deceased was wounded by a pistol bullet in the belly, and lived about twenty-four hours after. He declared to two eminent surgeons, who attended him, and to several other persons, that Mr. Donovan behaved, during the action, and after it, with the greatest honour, tenderness, and concern. And he particularly desired, that no prosecution should be carried on against him, as he himself was solely in fault, by an unprovoked rashness of temper, and heat of passion.

The learned Judge gave an excellent charge to the jury, and said, " Though he allowed that all the circumstances were as favourable to the prisoner, as in such a case could be; yet, as the idea of honour was so often mentioned, he must say, and inform the jury, and the auditors, that it was false honour in men to break the laws of God and their country: that going out to fight a duel, was, in both parties, a deliberate resolution to commit murder, and there could be no honour in so savage a custom, which, however disguised in words, is contrary to the principles and happiness of society, and ought to be reprobated in every well-regulated community."

The jury, without going out of court, acquitted Mr. Donovan of the murder, and found him " guilty" of " manslaughter," on the Coroner's Inquest. The Judge fined him ten pounds to the King, which being paid in the court, he was immediately discharged.

26.

Duel between the Rev. Mr. BATE *and Mr.* R——, *a Student of the Law. September* 7, 1780.

THIS morning about half-past four o'clock, a duel was fought in Hyde Park, between the Rev. Mr. Bate, of Surrey Street, and Mr. R——, a Student of the Law, late of St. John's College, Cambridge.

The quarrel arose from some circumstances relating to the conduct of the Morning Post, in which they are both engaged. The chance of the first fire falling to Mr. Bate, he discharged his pistol, and hit Mr. R—— in the fleshy part of the right arm. The wound, however, was not sufficient to incapacitate him from returning the fire, which he did, but without effect.

The seconds now interfered, and the affair was adjusted.

27.

Duel between the Rev. Mr. ALLEN *and* LLOYD DULANY, *Esq.* *June* 26, 1782.

DIED, in Park Street, Grosvenor Square, Lloyd Dulany, Esq. a gentleman of a most respectable character, and large property in Maryland.

His death is said to be occasioned by a wound, which he received on Tuesday evening last, in a duel with the Rev. Mr. Allen, in Hyde Park. The second of the former was — Delancey, Esq. and of the latter, Robert Morris, Esq. He was attended by Dr. Millman, and Messrs. Pott and Adair. The Magistrates of Bow Street having advertised a reward of ten guineas each, for the apprehension of the Rev. Mr. Allen, and Robert Morris, Esq. they were, in consequence, apprehended, and committed to Tothill Fields Bridewell.

July 6, 1782.

Yesterday the Rev. Mr. Allen surrendered himself at the Sessions House, in the Old Bailey, when he, and Robert Morris, Esq. were indicted for the " Wilful Murder," of Lloyd Dulany, Esq.

Mr. Justice Buller, in his charge to the jury, observed, that the case before them consisted of two parts, law and fact. As to law, there is not, nor ever was a doubt, that where two persons meet together deliberately to fight a duel, and one of them is killed, the other is guilty of " murder," and his second likewise. In respect to the fact, he stated, that the quarrel arose from a circumstance of three years standing. A paragraph called, " Characters of Principal men in Rebellion," published in the Morning Post, June 29, 1779, referred to the first and fifth of July, the same year, and now recognised by the prisoner Allen, in a letter proved to be his hand writing, avowing himself the author of those characters, retorting the charge of " liar and assassin," upon the deceased; telling him he did not mean to dispute with, but to punish him: and if he (the deceased) harboured any resentment, or revenge, the bearer (Morris) would put him in the way of securing its immediate execution. This brought on sundry verbal messages; and at last, on the 18th of June, a meeting of Mr. Dulany, Mr. Delancey, his second, and Mr. Morris: from which, they went to Mr. Wogden's, gun-maker, to get Mr. Allen's pistols charged; and about half-past nine in the evening, after measuring eight yards, discharged their pistols, when the deceased fell.

Mr. Delancey said, that Mr. Morris repeatedly urged deferring the duel to the next day.

One Lydia Lepine deposed, that she saw the prisoner Allen shooting at a mark, in a field near Blackfriars Bridge, with pistols, between eleven and twelve o'clock, on the 18th of June. Her master and his son confirmed the fact; but could not swear positively to the person. His

Lordship concluded with observing, that a mistaken point of honour was not to bias the judges and the jury in such a case.

The jury withdrew about twenty minutes, and brought in a verdict, Allen, " Guilty of Manslaughter." Morris, " Not Guilty." The Recorder, then, after a pathetic speech, pronounced sentence on Mr. Allen, of one shilling fine, and to be imprisoned six months in Newgate.

Bamber Gascoigne, Esq. and two ladies, proved an alibi as to shooting at a mark; and they, as well as Lords Bateman, Mountmorris, and several other persons, gave Allen an excellent character. Mr. Morris brought no witnesses.

28.

Duel prevented. March 9, 1783.

Two officers of the army, with their seconds, and a surgeon, met in a field near Kensington Gravel Pits, to fight a duel, but were happily prevented by the interposition of a clergyman, who lives in that neighbourhood, who happened to be passing by as they alighted from their carriages, and who suspecting their intention, interfered. The polite and affectionate address of this clergyman effected an honourable reconciliation.

29.

Duel between Mr. RIDDELL *and Mr.* CUNNINGHAM. *April* 21, 1783.

A duel was fought between Mr. Riddell, of the Horse Grenadiers, and Mr. Cunningham, of the Scots Greys. Both these gentlemen belonged formerly to the Scots Greys, and had differed at play. Mr. Riddell had challenged Mr. Cunningham, which challenge Mr. Cunningham had declined; but many of the gentlemen of the Scots Greys, reviving, at intervals, that circumstance, Mr. Cunningham found it necessary, for the full restoration of his honour, that he should call upon Mr. Riddell. This appeal, Mr. Riddell considering as out of season, declined attending to, till he had consulted his brother officers, who agreed, there was no obligation on him to answer Mr. Cunningham.

This being their determination, Mr. Cunningham resolved upon forcing him to the point, and meeting him accidentally at Mr. Christie's, their Agent, spate in his face. Mr. Riddell observed that this being a fresh affront, he should take notice of it, and took his departure. He then proceeded to make a few arrangements in his affairs. But before he had completed them, he received a billet from Mr. Cunningham, reminding him of the affront which he had passed upon him, and declaring his readiness to give him satisfaction. This note coming while the wafer was yet wet, to the hands of Sir James Riddell, who was under some apprehension of his son's situation, opened it, and having read it, closed it, without taking any other notice of its contents, than providing, in consequence of it, the assistance of several surgeons of the first abilities. The meeting was fixed. They were both punctual, Mr. Riddell attended by Captain Topham, of the Horse Grenadiers, and Mr. Cunningham by Captain Cunningham of the 69th regiment of foot.

Eight paces were first measured by the

seconds, and afterwards the contending parties took their ground. They tossed up for the first fire, which Mr. Riddell won. Mr. Riddell fired, and shot Mr. Cunningham under the right breast, the ball passing, as is supposed, through the ribs, and lodging on the left side near the back. The moment Mr. Cunningham received the shot, he reeled, but did not fall. He opened his waistcoat, and declared he was mortally wounded. Mr. Riddell still remained on his ground, when Mr. Cunningham, after a pause of two minutes, declared he would not be taken off the field till he had fired at his adversary. Mr. Cunningham then presented his pistol, and shot Mr. Riddell in the groin; he immediately fell, and was carried in a hackney coach to Mr. Topham's. The unhappy man lingered until seven o'clock on Tuesday morning, and then expired.

Wednesday, 23.

THE Coroner's Inquest sate on the body of George Riddell, Esq. who was killed in the rencontre, as above related.

The jury sate four hours; and after a

very strict examination of the seconds, and a servant of the deceased, brought in their verdict, "Manslaughter."

30.

Duel between Captain I. *and Colonel* P—.
June, 1783.

On the 31st ult. a duel was fought near Bangor Ferry, Caernarvonshire, between Captain I. and Colonel P——. In consequence of several disputes that had happened relating to the Anglesea militia, and a challenge given, some time ago, by Captain I. to Colonel P. they were bound over to preserve the peace for a year. That time being expired, Captain I. sent a message, that he should be at the Ferry house at six o'clock on Saturday morning, attended by Captain M. The parties met. The seconds marked the ground at twelve paces, and tossed up for the first fire, which Colonel P. gained. He fired, and shot Captain I. in the right thigh, who strove to return the fire, but his pistol missed. Captain I. then demanded a second shot; which not being immediately complied with, he was unable to bear longer on his thigh, and was carried off by the assistance of the seconds. There are hopes of his recovery.

31.

Duel between the Hon. Colonel COSMO GORDON *and Lieut-Colonel* THOMAS. *September* 4, 1783.

AT six this morning, the Hon. Col. Cosmo Gordon and Lieut.-Colonel Thomas, met at the Ring in Hyde-Park, to fight a duel. It was agreed upon by their seconds, that after receiving their pistols they should advance, and fire when they pleased. On arriving within about eight yards of each other they presented, and drew their triggers nearly at the same time, when only the Colonel's pistol went off. The Lieut.-Colonel having adjusted his pistol, fired at the Colonel, who received a severe contusion on the thigh. Their second pistols were fired without effect, and their friends called to reload them; after which they again advanced to nearly the same distance, and fired, when the Lieut.-Colonel fell, having received a ball in his body. He received immediate assistance from a surgeon, who attended the Colonel in case of need, and who extracted the ball on the field, which notwithstanding proved mortal.

32.

Duel between Mr. Monro, *of the* 16*th Regiment of Dragoons, and Mr.* Green. *October* 17, 1783.

This morning, about seven o'clock, Mr. Monro, of the 16th Regiment of Dragoons, and Mr. Green, with their seconds, met in a field near Battersea bridge, for the purpose of settling a dispute which took place a few evenings ago. They took their ground at the distance of about six yards. They then fired three pistols each, the last of which wounded Mr. Green in the side: The seconds interfered, and asked Mr. Green if he was satisfied. He said, " Not except Mr. Monro made him a public apology." " That," Mr. Monro said, " he *now* would not do. Mr. Green replied, " Then one of us must fall." They again took their ground, and fired each two pistols more. One ball entered Mr. Monro's knee, and Mr. Green received a shot which has since proved fatal, the ball entering a little above the groin.

33.

Duel between Lieutenant Harrison *and* M. Harman Van Berkensham. *October*, 1783.

This afternoon a duel was fought behind the Foundling Hospital, between Lieutenant Harrison, of the marines, and M. Harman Van Berkensham, an officer in the Dutch service. When, after marking out the distance of eight paces, Mr. Berkensham fired first and missed. Lieutenant Harrison's bullet grazed the cheek of his antagonist, who insisted on firing again, which he did without effect; and Lieutenant Harrison fired his second pistol into the air. The seconds interposed, the parties were reconciled, and both went home good friends.

34.

Duel between Sir JAMES LOWTHER *and Sergeant* BOLTON. *April*, 1784.

A duel was fought in this month between Sir James Lowther, and Sergeant Bolton, when three pistols were discharged on each side, but no material injury was done to either of the combatants; and the seconds interposing, they were reconciled.

35.

Duel between an Officer of the Navy and a German Officer. August, 1784.

AN Officer in the navy, and a Gentleman in the German service, fought a duel with swords and pistols, in a field near Bayswater. Four pistols were discharged, one of which slightly wounded the former in the left shoulder; but in the rencontre with swords, the latter was run through the thigh. A surgeon, who attended, stopped the effusion of blood, which was great; and the gentleman was taken to his apartments in Dean-street, dangerously ill.

This, it appears, is the second duel which these gentlemen have fought. The first was in France, where they were both desperately wounded. The quarrel was a difference of opinion on the conduct of General Burgoyne, in the Hudson's Bay expedition, in which they both served.

36.

Duel between Captain BRISES *and Captain* BULKLEY. *February,* 1785.

A duel was fought between Captains Brises and Bulkley. The first fire being won by the latter, he shot, and narrowly missed his antagonist, who fired his pistol in the air; and the seconds interposing, the affair ended in the field.

37.

Duel between Lieutenant F. *and Mr.* GORDON. *March,* 1785.

A duel was fought between Lieut. F., son of General F., then quartered in the Old Barracks at Chatham, and a gentleman of the name of Gordon, who was on a visit to his brother, an officer in the same barracks; when Mr. Gordon was so desperately wounded in one of his legs, that amputation became necessary. The affair took its rise in a quarrel at cards.

38.

Duel between Lord Macartney *and Mr.* Sadleir. *April*, 1785.

The duel between Lord Macartney and Mr. Sadleir, which was at first thought unfounded, appears to have been a serious business. They, with their seconds, Mr. Davidson and Major Grattan, took their ground about seven o'clock in the morning, on the 24th of September, 1784. The distance marked by the seconds was ten paces. The lot to fire first fell to Mr. Sadleir; who firing accordingly, the ball struck Lord Macartney on the ribs of the left side, which was not known to the seconds till after his Lordship had likewise fired without effect. It had been previously agreed between the seconds, after the first fire, if no material execution had been done, to interpose their good offices to effect a reconciliation. This they were about to do, when it was discovered that Lord Macartney had been wounded. When the previous agreement was mentioned to his Lordship, and he was asked his sentiments, his answer was—" That he came there to give Mr. Sadleir satisfaction, and he was still ready to do so." And Mr. Sadleir being told that Lord Macartney was wounded, and that, in the present circumstances, the affair could not honourably be pursued any farther, he acquiesced, and declared that he was satisfied. And thus the affair ended.

39.
Duel between the EARL *of* A. *and Mr.* F. M. *June* 19, 1785.

THIS day a duel was fought, near Grosvenor Gate, between the Right Hon. the Earl of A., of the kingdom of Ireland, and Mr. F. M., of the same kingdom.

The affair happened from a punctilio of honour. After they had taken their ground, both attempted to fire at the same time; but his Lordship's pistol missing fire, and

Mr. M.'s shot not taking effect, the affair ended to the satisfaction of all parties.

19.

Duel between COMTE DE GERSDORFF *and* Mons. LOUIS LE FAVRE. *July*, 1785.

A challenge was circulated through Europe by the public prints, from Comte de Gersdorff to Mons. Louis Le Favre; the former of whom offered a hundred louis d'ors to the latter, to bear his charges to any place which he might appoint for the meeting. To this challenge Mons. Le Favre afterwards published the following answer.

Filbourg, April 28, 1785.

MONS. LE COMTE,

I hasten to answer your circular letter inserted in the public prints. Our interview, if you think proper, shall be at B— le D—. As I am in the neighbourhood of the city, I do not want much money to carry me thither; and I thank you sincerely for the hundred louis which you offer me. I have the honour to be, &c. &c.

LE FAVRE.

The Comte in his replication pleads indisposition. But the parties at length met; and there never was such a farce of a fight. Their seconds measured the ground at twenty-five paces. The heroes took their stations, fired a pistol or two each. Their seconds commended their bravery: the Comte forgave the Secretary, and there was an end of the combat.

41.

Duel between Lord William Murray *and Mr.* Gilbert Waugh. *November* 1785.

By the East India packet, advice was received of a duel fought between Lord William Murray, and Lieutenant Gilbert Waugh, of the Seventy-third Regiment, on the 21st of October, 1784, in which the latter was mortally wounded, and died three days after, greatly regretted.

42.

Duel between Lieutenant Gamble *and Lieutenant* Mollison. *January* 1786.

A duel was fought at Chatham Lines, between Lieutenant Gamble and Lieutenant Mollison, both of them of the Marines. No compromise could be settled by the seconds, and Lieutenant Mollison firing first, hit his antagonist in the upper part of his thigh. Lieutenant Gamble fell, but suddenly starting up, as Mr. Mollison advanced towards him, discharged his pistol, and the ball shattered the humerus or upper bone of Mr. Mollison's arm, a little above the elbow. Here the seconds interposed, and the combatants were taken into their quarters. Mr. Mollison's arm has since been amputated, and both the gentlemen are now perfectly reconciled, and as good friends as ever.

43.

Duel between LORD MACARTNEY *and Major General* STEWART. *June* 8, 1786.

A duel was fought near Kensington, between Lord Macartney and Major General Stewart, of which the following is an authentic account.

The place and time of meeting having

been previously fixed, the parties arrived about half-past four in the morning, and took their ground at the distance of twelve short paces, measured off by the seconds, who delivered to each one pistol, keeping possession of the remaining arms.

General Stewart told Lord Macartney, he doubted, as his lordship was short-sighted, he would not be able to see him. His lordship replied, "he did perfectly well." When the seconds had retired a little on one side, and as the parties were about to level, General Stewart observed to Lord Macartney, that his pistol was not cocked: His lordship thanked him, and cocked. When they had levelled, General Stewart said, "he was ready." His lordship answered, "he was likewise ready." And they both fired within a few instants of each other. The seconds observing Lord Macartney wounded, stepped up to him, and declared the matter must rest here. General Stewart said, "this is no satisfaction." And asked if his lordship was not able to fire another pistol. His lordship replied, "he would try with pleasure," and urged Colonel Fullarton to permit him to proceed. The seconds, however, declared it was impossible, and they would on no account allow it. General Stewart said, "then I must defer it till another occasion;" on which his lordship answered, " if that be the case, we had better proceed now. I am here in consequence of a mes- from General Stewart, who called upon me to give him satisfaction in my private capa- city, for offence taken at my public con- duct; and to evince that personal safety is no consideration with me, I have nothing personal: the General may proceed as he thinks fit." General Stewart said, "It was his lordship's personal conduct to him that he resented."

The seconds then put an end to all fur- ther conversation between the parties, neither of whom had quitted their ground; General Stewart, in consequence of his si- tuation, having been under the necessity, from the first, of putting his back to a tree. The surgeons, Mr. Hunter and Mr. Home, and who were attending at a little distance, were brought up by Colonel Fullarton. Colonel Gordon, in the mean time, assisted his lordship in taking off his coat, and requested him to sit down, apprehending he might be faint through loss of blood. Colonel Gordon then left the ground, in company with General Stewart, and an easy carriage was provided to convey his lordship home.

(Signed)   W. FULLARTON,
A. GORDON.

44.

Duel between Counsellor HUTCHINSON *and* LORD MOUNTMORRIS. *May,* 1787.

ON the 28th ult. a duel took place between Counsellor Hutchinson, third son to the Provost of the University of Dublin, and Lord Mountmorris, in consequence of some words spoken by the latter in the House of Lords, on Monday the 23rd of April, of which his lordship refused to give an explanation.

The parties met at Donnybrook; and the seconds having measured the ground, both fired at the same instant: when Lord Mountmorris fell, in consequence of a wound under the arm, and the seconds interposed to prevent farther bloodshed.

45.

Duel between Chevalier LA B. *and Captain* S. *June,* 1787.

ABOUT three in the morning, on the 10th, a duel was fought between the Chevalier La B. an officer in the French service, and Captain S. of the 11th Regiment of foot. The ground measured, was five paces, and the first shot that was fired by Captain S. took place on the Chevalier's breast, but was fortunately prevented from penetrating by the intervention of his coat button; on which he fired his pistol into the air. The seconds interposed, and the combatants parted friends. The expression for which Captain S. called out the Chevalier, was to this effect: " That the English army had more *phlegm* than *spirit*."

46.

Duel between Sir JOHN MACPHERSON *and Major* BROWNE. *September* 10, 1787.

A duel took place in Hyde Park, between Sir John Macpherson, and Major Browne.

The parties met near Grosvenor Gate, about eleven o'clock. The pistols were loaded on the ground, and it was agreed they both should fire at the same time. They did so. Sir John received the Major's second fire; but his own pistol missed fire. Colonel Murray, second to Sir John, then asked Major Roberts, who was second to Major Browne, " if his friend was satisfied." Major Browne said, " he was satisfied that Sir John had behaved with great gallantry, and much like a man of honour." But some further explanation being required on the part of the Major, a third shot was exchanged. And, then, both parties quitting the ground, came up to each other, said a few words, and parted with salutations of civility.

47.

Dublin, January 31, 1788.

THIS day Robert Keon, Esq. was brought up to the Court of King's Bench, to receive sentence for the murder of George Nugent Reynolds, Esq.

The circumstances of this murder were

the following : These two gentlemen went out to fight a duel, and when Mr. Reynolds, previous to coming to action, was in the act of saluting Mr. Keon with his hat in his hand, wishing him a good morning, the latter fired his pistol, and shot him through the head. Upon this, Mr. Plunket, Mr. Reynolds's second, called out, " A horrid murder!" On which Mr. Keon's brother replied, " If you don't like it, take that," and snapped his pistol at Mr. Plunket, which luckily did not go off. The jury found Mr. Keon, " guilty," in November last; but his counsel moved an arrest of judgment, and pleaded several errors in the different proceedings, to stop the sentence. The court, after the most solemn arguments, over-ruled all the objections, and passed sentence of death upon him, according to the verdict, and he was executed on the sixteenth of the following month.

48.

Duel between His Royal Highness the DUKE OF YORK *and Colonel* LENOX. *May,* 1789.

ON the 17th instant, a duel took place between the Duke of York and Colonel Lenox. Lord Rawdon was second to the Duke of York, and the Earl of Winchilsea to Colonel Lenox.

The dispute originated in an expression of the Duke of York, " that Colonel Lenox had heard words spoken to him at Daubigny's, to which no gentleman ought to have submitted." This observation being repeated to Colonel Lenox, he took the opportunity, while His Royal Highness was on the parade, to address him, desiring to know, what were the words, which he submitted to hear, and by whom they were spoken. To this His Royal Highness gave no other answer, than by ordering him to his post. The parade being over, His Royal Highness went into the Orderly Room, and sending for the Colonel, intimated to him, in the presence of all the officers, that he desired to derive no protection from his rank as a prince, and his station as commanding officer: but that, when not on duty, he wore a brown coat, and was ready, as a private gentleman, to give the Colonel satisfaction.

After this declaration, Colonel Lenox wrote a circular letter to every member of the club at Daubigny's, requesting to know whether such words had been used to him, and appointing a particular day for an answer from each; their silence to be considered as a declaration that no such words could be recollected.

On the expiration of the term limited for an answer to the circular letter, the Colonel sent a written message to His Royal Highness to this purport—" That not being able to recollect any occasion on which words had been spoken to him at Daubigny's, to which a gentleman ought not to submit, he had taken the step which had appeared to him most likely to gain information of the words to which His Royal Highness had alluded, and of the person who had used them: that none of the members of the club had given him information of any such insult being in their knowledge; and therefore he expected, in justice to his character, that His Royal Highness should contradict the report as publicly as he had asserted it."

This letter was delivered to His Royal Highness by the Earl of Winchilsea; when the answer returned not proving satisfactory, a message was sent to His Royal Highness desiring a meeting; and the time and place were settled that evening.

The meeting took place on Wimbledon Common. The Duke of York received Colonel Lenox's fire, but did not fire himself; the ball from Colonel Lenox grazed His Royal Highness's curl.

Some days after this, Colonel Lenox made a requisition to the Duke of York, as Colonel of the Coldstream Regiment, that His Royal Highness would permit a call of the officers of that corps, in order that certain propositions touching his conduct and situation might be submitted to their consideration.

His Royal Highness informed the friend of Mr. Lenox, "That he could not possibly oppose any design which might tend to relieve Mr. Lenox from his present embarrassment." The meeting of this military convention was held yesterday at the Orderly Room, at two o'clock, and after a considerable deliberation, the meeting adjourned over to the 1st of June, at one; when, after a considerable discussion, the Convention came to the following resolution:—" It is the opinion of the Coldstream Regiment, that subsequent to the 15th of May, the day of the meeting at the Orderly Room, Lieut.-Colonel Lenox has behaved with courage, but, from the peculiar difficulty of his situation, not with judgment."

Colonel Lenox soon after exchanged his company in the Duke of York's regiment, for the commission of Lieut.-Colonel in the 35th Regiment of Foot.

49.

Duel between Captain EDWARD PELLEW *and Lieutenant* I. M. NORTHEY. *June,* 1789.

A duel was fought at Exeter, on Tuesday the 9th, in consequence of a previous dispute, between Captain Edward Pellew, of the navy, and Lieutenant I. M. Northey. The former was attended to the field by Captain Reynolds; the latter by his brother, Thomas Northey, Esq. The parties took their ground at twelve paces; and a signal being given, they both fired, when Lieutenant Northey's ball passed through his opponent's coat. A second signal being given, as agreed, both parties reserved their fire. An explanation between the friends took place, and the matter was settled to the satisfaction and honour of all parties. To prevent misrepresentation, the foregoing account is published by the seconds.

50.

Duel between Captain TONGUE *and Captain* PATERSON. *June* 19, 1789.

A duel was fought between Captain Tongue, of His Majesty's Sixth Regiment, and Captain Paterson, in the East India Company's military service, in which Captain Tongue was wounded in the side.

The cause of the quarrel originated in the street. Captain Tongue acknowledged himself the aggressor.

51.

Duel between Colonel LENOX *and* THEOPHILUS SWIFT, *Esq.* *July* 1, 1789.

THIS evening, in consequence of some expressions reflecting on the character of Lieut.-Colonel Lenox, published in a pamphlet, with the name of Theophilus Swift, Esq. Colonel Lenox called on Mr. Swift, and demanded satisfaction.

They met in a field near the Uxbridge road, attended by Sir William Augustus Browne and Lieut.-Colonel Phipps. Ten paces were measured by the seconds; and it was agreed that Lieut.-Colonel Lenox should fire first. The parties having taken their ground, Colonel Lenox asked, if Mr. Swift was ready? On his answering that he was, Colonel Lenox fired, and the ball took place in the body of Mr. Swift, whose pistol, on his receiving the wound, went off without effect. The parties then quitted the ground.

It is but just to say, that both gentlemen behaved with the utmost degree of coolness and intrepidity. Mr. Swift has since recovered from his wound.

52.

Duel between —— CURRAN, *Esq.*, M. P. *and Major* HOBART. *April* 1, 1790.

A duel was fought in Luttrelstown, between —— Curran, Esq., M. P., and Major Hobart, secretary to the Lord Lieutenant, occasioned by some words spoken in Parliament.

The meeting was at the Hermitage, one of Lord Carhampton's seats. Mr. Curran was attended by Mr. Egan, Major Hobart by Lord Carhampton. Being put to their ground, and having agreed to fire as they chose, Mr. Curran fired first, without effect; whereupon Major Hobart said, "He hoped Mr. Curran was satisfied." Mr. Egan then called out to Major Hobart that he had not fired, as did Mr. Curran. The Major advancing a step or two towards Mr. Curran, repeated what he had said before. Mr. Curran replied, "I am sorry, Sir, you have taken this advantage: but you have made it impossible for me not to be satisfied."

53.

Duel between Sir GEORGE RAMSAY *and Captain* MACRAE. *Edinburgh, April,* 15, 1790.

A duel was fought yesterday near this city. The parties were Sir George Ramsay and Captain Macrae. The circumstances are as follow:—

A servant of Sir George's, keeping a chair at the door of the Edinburgh Theatre, was ordered by Captain Macrae to remove it. On his objecting, some words ensued; and the fracas concluded in Captain Macrae chastising the servant very severely.

Meeting the next day with Sir George Ramsay, he insisted on his dismissing the man from his service. This was refused, on the ground, that whatever was the misconduct of the servant, he had already received a sufficient punishment.

A challenge was the immediate consequence of this refusal. The parties met on Musselbrough Links, Sir George Ramsay accompanied by Sir William Maxwell, and Captain Macrae by Mr. Hay.

The former fired first, but without effect;

Captain Macrae returned the fire, and lodged his ball near the heart of his antagonist. Sir George languished in much agony until Friday morning, when he expired. He was a gentleman of the most amiable character and disposition; and had but lately married a beautiful young lady, the sister of Lord Saltoun.

Captain Macrae and his second immediately fled. The poor fellow, on whose account this duel happened, no sooner heard of his master's fate, than he fell into strong convulsions, and died in the course of a few hours.

July, 1790.

ON Monday the High Court of Justiciary met at Edinburgh, for the trial of James Macrae, of Hollmains, indicted at the instance of the Hon. Lady Ramsay, and Sir William Ramsay, of Bamff, Bart., and of His Majesty's Advocate, for the murder of the late Sir George Ramsay, Bart., on the 14th of April last. Mr. Macrae not having appeared, to stand trial, sentence of fugitation (outlawry) was pronounced against him.

54.

Duel between Mr. STEPHENS *and Mr.* ANDERSON. *Margate, Sept.* 21, 1790.

YESTERDAY a duel was fought at Kingsgate, between Mr. Stephens, son of Philip Stephens, Esq., secretary to the Admiralty, and a Mr. Anderson.

It originated in such a trifling circumstance as a dispute about the shutting of a window in the public rooms. The parties fired each a pistol without effect; but at the second fire, Mr. Anderson's ball entered between Mr. Stephens's under lip and chin, and passing to the jugular vein in the neck, occasioned his almost instantaneous death.

Mr. Anderson was apprehended soon after; and this day the coroner's inquest sate on the body, and brought in their verdict, " Manslaughter."

The bill of indictment afterwards presented against Mr. Anderson for murder, in his unhappy meeting with Stephens, was unanimously thrown out, as frivolous and unfounded, by the grand jury at Dover.

55.

Duel between Captain HARVEY ASTON *and Lieutenant* FITZGERALD. *June* 25, 1790.

A duel was fought between Captain Harvey Aston and Lieutenant Fitzgerald, of the 60th Regiment of foot. The cause of the dispute happened at Ranelagh, but so long before the challenge, that it was imagined all idea of hostility had ceased. A field belonging to Chalk Lodge Farm, near Hampstead, was the chosen spot, and break of day, the time appointed. Lord Charles Fitzroy was the second to Captain Aston, and Mr. Hood was second to Lieutenant Fitzgerald.

Ten yards was the ground measured; and Mr. Fitzgerald had the first fire. He rested his pistol on the left arm, and took aim accordingly. The ball took a direction, so as to glance on Mr. Aston's wrist, and passed from thence under his right cheek bone, and through the neck. On receiving this wound, Captain Aston called to his antagonist; "Are you satisfied." The answer returned was, "I am satisfied." Captain Aston then retired from the ground, and was assisted to his carriage. Happily the wound is not likely to prove mortal.

56.

Duel between Mr. GRAHAM *and Mr.*
JULIUS. *July* 19, 1791.

AN unfortunate rencontre took place this morning, upon Blackheath, between Mr. Graham, an eminent special pleader, of the Temple, and Mr. Julius, a pupil in the office of Messrs. Grahams, Attorneys, of Lincoln's Inn, who are brothers of the former.

The parties had dined together, at the house of Mr. Black, the Surveyor, upon Epping Forest, on Sunday: and after dinner, having drank freely, the latter expressing some free opinions concerning religion, much abrupt language passed between them. They were reconciled, however, on that day, and returned to town in the same carriage.

On Monday, they met again after dinner, at the chambers of Mr. Graham, Lincoln's Inn, the brother of the deceased, where the dispute was unfortunately renewed, though apparently without malignity. No challenge was given that night. But in the morning, the deceased called upon Mr. Julius for an apology, for some expressions;

which being refused, they went out together, Mr. Graham attended by Mr. Ellis, and Mr. Julius by Mr. Maxwell. A pupil of an eminent surgeon attended them to Blackheath, where Mr. Graham fell by a shot which passed almost through the lower part of the belly. He was brought to town in a post chaise, and the exertions of the most eminent of the faculty were, in vain, used for his relief; the ball having laid open the femoral artery, and it being impossible to stop the discharge of blood, he expired in the afternoon of the next day.

Mr. Graham was a gentleman of considerable eminence in his profession, and of an esteemed character in private life.

Mr. Julius is the son of a very respectable attorney at St. Kitt's, and is said not to have been the least to blame in this quarrel.

57.

Duel between Mr. FRIZELL *and Mr.* CLARK. *June*, 1792.

A duel was yesterday morning fought in Hyde Park, between Mr. Frizell and Mr.

Clark, both students of the law. Mr. Montgomery was second to Mr. Frizell, and Mr. Evans to Mr. Clark.

On Thursday night, these four gentlemen were in company at the Cecil Street Coffee House, where Mr. Frizell lodged. They drank till one in the morning, when Mr. Frizell declaring he could drink no longer, Mr. Clark said, with some warmth, " It was using his friends very ill, but that it was not the first time he had behaved so; for that at Chatham, he had quarrelled with all the officers, and particularly with his friend Lieutenant Hixon, of the 14th Regiment, and that he had the character of a fighting man." Mr. Frizell replied, " That he did not mean to give offence, but if any thing that he had said, could be so construed, he was ready to give Mr. Clark satisfaction," and then went to bed.

Mr. Clark insisted, that these words were a direct challenge, and appealed to the other gentlemen, who declared, that they did not consider them in that light. Mr. Clark, however, went up to Mr. Frizell's room, and insisted on his meeting him in five minutes. Mr. Frizell immediately dressed himself, and went down stairs, where he said, before all the parties, that if Mr. Evans and Mr. Montgomery were of opinion that he had been guilty of any improper conduct, he would apologize for it to Mr. Clark. But that gentleman said, " he would accept of no apology," and insisted, that he should meet him in Hyde Park, in an hour from the time, three o'clock.

It was then settled that Mr. Evans and Mr. Montgomery should be the seconds. And after these gentlemen had in vain endeavoured to make up the difference, Mr. Clark, accompanied by Mr. Evans, went out for pistols. Mr. Clark procured a brace, which he loaded, and observing that Mr. Frizell had not got pistols, gave him one of his.

When they got to the ground, they stood at the distance of ten yards, and tossed up for the first fire, which was won by Mr. Clark, whose ball penetrated Mr. Frizell's collar-bone. He fell, and as he was falling, his pistol went off. Mr. Montgomery, not supposing him dead, ran for a coach, to convey him to a surgeon's; but, on his return, found Mr. Frizell had expired. Mr. Clark and Mr. Evans were standing by the body, and were surrounded by some soldiers, who refused to let them go, until their serjeant came to them. The serjeant (who had previously been to Knightsbridge Barracks, to consult his officer, Captain Hill, what was to be done) presently appeared, and set them at liberty; when the body was put into a coach, into which they all got, and drove off. In Piccadilly, Mr. Clark and Mr. Evans got out, and have not since been heard of.

Mr. Frizell and Mr. Clark were natives of Ireland, as were the two seconds. They were all young men. The Coroner's Inquest has since sate on the body of Mr. Frizell, and brought in their verdict, "wilful murder."

58.

Duel between Mr. KEMBLE *and Mr.* AIKIN, *March* 1792.

A duel was fought, in a field near Mary-le-bone, between Mr. Kemble and Mr. Aikin, of Drury Lane Theatre, in consequence of a dispute respecting certain dramatical arrangements, which Mr. Aikin conceived to be injurious to him.

Mr. Aikin discharged his pistol without effect, and the parties were happily reconciled without proceding further. They had no seconds; but Mr. Bannister, Sen. attended, as their common friend.

59.

Duel between the EARL OF LONSDALE *and Captain* CUTHBERT, *of the Guards. June* 9, 1792.

AN affair of honour took place, early this morning, between the Earl of Lonsdale, and Captain Cuthbert, of the Guards, which, after the discharge of a brace of pistols, on each side, terminated without injury to either party. Lord Lonsdale's last shot would, probably, have been fatal, if the ball had not luckily struck a button of Captain Cuthbert, which repelled it. The seconds then interfered, and matters were amicably adjusted. The circumstances, which led to this hazardous decision, were as follow:

Captain Cuthbert, in order to obviate all increasing disturbance in Mount Street, had directed that no carriage should be suffered to pass that way. Lord Lonsdale, who came in his carriage to Mount Street, was consequently obstructed; and, finding the impediment insuperable, his temper was somewhat ruffled. Addressing himself, therefore, to Captain Cuthbert, he exclaimed, " You r—s—l, do you know that I am a peer of the realm?" The Captain immediately replied, " I don't know that you are a peer, but I know you are a s—d—l, for applying such a term to an officer on duty; and I will make you answer for it." A meeting, of course, took place, and concluded as stated.

60.

Duel between Lord Lauderdale *and General* Arnold. *July* 2, 1792.

Lord Lauderdale, attended by the Right Honourable Charles James Fox, and General Arnold, with Lord Hawke as his friend, had a meeting near Kilburn Wells, to terminate a misunderstanding, which it was found impossible to conciliate.

Lord Lauderdale received the General's fire unhurt, when, his lordship declining to return the shot, the seconds retired for about ten minutes, and the result was the finishing of the affair. The noble Earl, upon being desired to fire, observed, that he did not come there to fire at the General, nor could he retract the offensive expressions; if General Arnold was not satisfied, he might fire till he was. A like rencontre took place, a few days before, betweeen the noble Earl, and the Duke of Richmond.

61.

Duel between Mons. CHAUVIGNY *and Mons.* C. LAMETH. *November* 8, 1792.

A duel has taken place between Mons. Chauvigny and Mons. Charles Lameth. This affair, which originated in a difference of opinion, had been undecided for two years. It appears that M. de Chauvigny, having learned the arrival of his antagonist in this country, gave him a meeting, and proposed to fight him, which the latter assented to. The parties fought in a field near the place of Mons. Lameth's residence, and he was dangerously wounded in the belly. The affair ended by both declaring themselves satisfied, and giving their word of honour that the matter was finally adjusted.

The seconds were, for Mons. Chauvigny, the Duke de Pienne and the Count de Chabanc; and for Mons. Lameth, the Duke d'Aiguillon and Mr. Maselet.

62.

Duel between Mr. PUREFOY *and Colonel* ROPER. *Maidstone, August* 14, 1794.

AT our assizes this day, Mr. Thomas Purefoy was indicted for the "wilful murder" of Colonel Roper, in a duel, which took place on the 21st of December, 1788. The interval which had occurred between that time and the prosecution, was not assignable to the prosecutor, as Mr. Purefoy had, for the greater part of the time, been out of the kingdom.

In 1787, Major Roper was commander

in chief of the Island of St. Vincent, and Mr. Purefoy was Ensign in the 66th Regiment. The latter, having obtained leave of absence, had a festive day with some of the junior officers, in which they committed such excesses, as occasioned a complaint to Major Roper, by whom the leave of absence was recalled. The remonstrances of Mr. Purefoy were made in such a style, as to induce Major Roper to bring him to a court-martial. By their verdict, he was declared to have forfeited his commission; and this verdict was afterwards confirmed by His Majesty. This was the origin of the dispute, which had afterwards such a fatal termination.

The evidence, particularly that of General Stanwix, the second to Colonel Roper, was extremely favourable to the prisoner; who, being called upon for his defence, said, that he had entertained no malice against the deceased; he had been led by a call of honour, or, more properly speaking, driven by the tyranny of custom, to an act, which in early life had embittered his existence; but without which, he was taught to believe, that he should lose all the consideration which society could afford. The last challenge, he observed, had come from Colonel Roper; and, as some expiation of his offence, he had already suffered six years of exile, and nine months of close confinement. The latter part of this address was read from a written paper, by Mr. Erskine, the feelings of Mr. Purefoy being such as to overpower his utterance.

The prisoner called nine gentlemen to his character, most of whom had known him from early life. They all spoke to the general mildness of his character, and the good-humoured ease, and aversion to quarrel, which marked his general deportment. After a charge by the Judge, Mr. Baron Hotham, the jury, without hesitation, returned their verdict, " Not guilty."

63.

Duel between Major SWEETMAN *and Captain* WATSON. *January* 12, 1796.

IN consequence of a dispute at the Opera House, on Saturday evening, between Major Sweetman, of the Independants, and Captain Watson, of the 90th Regiment:

these gentlemen, attended by their seconds and surgeons, met yesterday morning near Cobham.

The combatants were posted by the seconds at the distance of ten yards; but Major Sweetman, who was short-sighted, complaining that he could not see clearly, Captain Watson called out to him to advance till he was satisfied: he advanced to within four yards, when both parties fired together. Captain Watson's ball went in at Major Sweetman's right breast, and came out at his left; he fell, and instantly expired. Captain Watson was wounded in the upper part of the thigh, but is in a fair way of recovery, the ball having been extracted.

March 20, 1796.

THIS day came on at Kingston assizes, the trial of Captain Brereton Watson, for the "murder" of Major Sweetman in a duel, which took place in January, at Cobham.

Captain Watson, still very ill of his wounds, was carried on a sofa covered with black into court. The surgeons refusing to be examined, through fear of being implicated in the crime with which the prisoner was charged, the trial was very short; and the result was, that Captain Watson was acquitted.

64.

Duel between Mr. Richard England *and Mr.* Rowlls. *February*, 19, 1796.

Mr. Richard England was put to the bar at the Old Bailey, charged with the "wilful murder" of Mr. Rowlls, Brewer, of Kingston, in a duel at Cranford Bridge, June 18th, 1784.

Lord Derby, the first witness, gave in evidence, that he was present at Ascot races. When in the stand upon the racecourse, he heard Mr. England cautioning the gentlemen present not to bet with the deceased, as he neither paid what he lost, nor what he borrowed. On which Mr. Rowlls went up to him, called him rascal, or scoundrel, and offered to strike him; when Mr. England bid him stand off, or he would be obliged to knock him down; saying, at the same time, "We have interrupted the company sufficiently here, and if you have any thing further to say to me, you know where I am to be found." A further altercation ensued, but his lordship being at the other end of the stand, did not distinctly hear it; and then the parties retired. Lord Dartrey, now Lord Cremorne, and his Lady, with a gentleman, were at the inn at the time the duel was fought. They went into the garden, and endeavoured to prevent the duel: several other persons were collected in the garden. Mr. Rowlls desired his lordship and others, not to interfere; and on a second attempt of his lordship to make peace, Mr. Rowlls said, if they did not retire, he must, though reluctantly, call them impertinent. Mr. England at the same time stepped forward, and took off his hat; he said, " Gentlemen, I have been cruelly treated; I have been injured in my honour and character; let reparation be made, and I am ready to have done this moment." Lady Dartrey retired. His lordship stood in the bower of the garden, until he saw Mr. Rowlls fall. One or two witnesses were called, who proved nothing material.

A paper, containing the Prisoner's defence, being read, the Earl of Derby, Marquis of Hertford, Mr. Whitbread, jun., Colonel Bishopp, and other gentlemen, were called to his character. They all spoke of him as a man of decent gentlemanly deportment, who, instead of seeking quarrels, was studious to avoid them. He had been friendly to Englishmen while abroad, and had rendered some service to the military at the siege of Newport.

Mr. Justice Rooke summed up the evidence; after which the jury retired for about three quarters of an hour, when they returned a verdict of "Manslaughter."

The prisoner having fled from the laws of his country for twelve years, the Court was disposed to shew no lenity. He was therefore sentenced to pay a fine of one shilling, and to be imprisoned in Newgate twelve months.

65.

Duel between LORD MALDEN *and the* DUKE OF NORFOLK. *April* 30, 1796.

IN consequence of a publication, addressed by Lord Malden to the inhabitants of the borough of Leominster, the Duke of Norfolk, accompanied by Captain Wombwell, of the First West York regiment of militia, and Lord Malden, accompanied by Captain Taylor, Aid-du-camp to His Royal Highness the Duke of York, met on Saturday morning, in a field beyond Paddington.

The parties having taken their ground, and the word being given by one of the seconds, they fired without effect. The seconds then thought proper to offer their interference; and in consequence of a conversation which passed while the parties were on the ground, a reconciliation was effected.

66.

Duel between LORD VALENTIA *and* HENRY GAWLER, *Esq. June* 28, 1796.

A duel was fought, in a field within three miles of Hamburgh, between Lord Valentia and Henry Gawler, Esq. They left England with their seconds and surgeons, for the express purpose of fighting. They fired together. Mr. Gawler's ball took place; it entered his lordship's breast bone, and lodged near the neck. It was extracted on the field; and he is considered to be out of danger. Lord Valentia's ball passed through Mr. Gawler's hat.

The affair between Mr. Gawler and Lady Valentia was the subject of the dispute.

67.

Duel between Mr. WILLIAM CARPENTER *and Mr.* JOHN PRIDE. *Aug.* 20, 1796.

THIS morning a duel was fought in Hyde-Park, between Mr. William Carpenter and Mr. John Pride, both Americans; in which Mr. Carpenter received his antagonist's ball in the side, which penetrated nearly through his body; and, notwithstanding it was immediately extracted, he died soon after.

The coroner's jury afterwards sate upon the body, and brought in their verdict, " wilful murder."

68.

Duel between Lieutenant FITZGERALD *and Lieutenant* WARRINGTON. *May* 4, 1797.

IN consequence of a quarrel which happened in the theatre, at Plymouth, on

Friday evening last, between Lieutenant Fitzgerald, of the marines, and Lieutenant Warrington of the 25th Regiment, they met on Sunday morning, accompanied by their seconds, to settle the business. They exchanged shots without effect; but on the second fire, Lieutenant Fitzgerald's ball wounded Lieutenant. Warrington in the side; after which the business terminated.

69.
Duel between Captain SMITH *and Lieutenant* FRANCIS BUCKLEY. *August 5, 1797.*

KILLED in a duel with Captain Smith, of the same regiment, Lieutenant Francis Buckley, of the Loyal British Fencibles, in the island of Jersey.

After exchanging several shots, the deceased received his antagonist's ball in his right side, and died almost instantly.

The cause of this unfortunate affair is said to have arisen from a quarrel between Captain Smith and the deceased; in which the former received a blow from the latter, who imagined that very improper language had been made use of towards him.

He has left a wife and two infant children, a brother (a lieutenant in the same regiment), and aged parents, to lament his untimely fate.

70.

Duel between Colonel KING *and Colonel* FITZGERALD. *October,* 1797.

ABOUT four weeks ago, the Hon. Miss King, who lived with her mother, Lady Kingsborough, eloped from Windsor. There were many circumstances attending the elopement, which led to a suspicion of the person who had seduced her from her duty.

Colonel Fitzgerald, who is married to a very beautiful lady, and is second cousin to Miss King, had been very attentive to her for some time; and, it appears, had previously found means to lead her astray. She was very young, being now only sixteen years of age; and her habits of life had been such, as to leave her more uninformed of the vicious habits of the world, than happens to most young people, even at that early age:

Colonel Fitzgerald was at length attacked

by her friends, as being accessory to her elopement. But he was, at first, extremely indignant, and threatened to fight any person who should accuse him. The afflicted parent, by the advice of friends, had, at length, recourse to the newspapers, and after having repeatedly advertised, in vain, for her daughter, was induced to offer a reward of a hundred guineas, for her recovery. It was, in consequence of the reward offered, that a young woman, daughter of the mistress of the house, where the young lady was concealed, in Clayton Street, Kennington, discovered Miss King and her seducer.

As soon as Lord Kingsborough, who was in Ireland, heard of the fate of his daughter, he came to England with his son, Colonel King; and, the first step was, to find out Colonel Fitzgerald, which was not done without some difficulty; as they were determined to call him to a personal and severe account.

Lord Kingsborough wrote to his friend, Major Wood, at Ashford, requesting his immediate attendance in town. As soon as he arrived, a meeting was appointed, and a duel took place, of which the following particulars are given by Major Wood to a friend.

Fladong's Hotel, Oxford Street, October 1, 1797.

MY DEAR FRIEND,

I shall, without preface, enter at once into the affair, which I mentioned to you was to take place this morning, " And nothing extenuate, nor set down aught in malice."

Agreeable to an arranged plan, I accompanied Colonel King to a spot near the Magazine in the Park. Colonel Fitzgerald we met at Grosvenor Gate, unaccompanied by a friend, which, by the way, he told me yesterday he feared he should not be able to provide, in consequence of the odium, which was thrown upon his character, at the same time observing, " That he was so sensible of my honour, that he was perfectly satisfied to meet Colonel King, unattended by a friend." I decidedly refused any interference on his part, informing him " That had not nearer relations of the —— been on the spot, he would have seen me as a principal." He replied, " He would try to procure a friend," and withdrew. I addressed him this morning by

" Where is your friend, Sir?" Answer (as well as I recollect) " I have not been able to procure one; I rest assured that you will act fairly." I then desired him to apply to his surgeon; which he immediately did, who refused appearing as a second, but said he would be in view, Colonel King was equally desirous to go on with the business. I consented. However, I prevailed upon a surgeon, who accompanied Dr. Browne, to be present as a witness that all was fairly conducted. It was no common business. I placed them at ten short paces distance from each other. That distance I thought too far. But I indulged a hope, that Colonel Fitzgerald, sensible of the vileness of his conduct, would, after the first fire, have thrown himself on Colonel King's humanity. His conduct was quite the reverse. In short, they exchanged six shots without effect. King was cool and determined. The other, also, determined; and, to appearance, obstinately bent on blood. After the fourth shot, he said something to me about giving him advice as a friend. I told him I was no friend of his, but that I was a friend to humanity, that, if after what had passed, he possessed firmness enough to ackowledge to Colonel King, that he was the vilest of human beings, and bear without reply any language from Colonel King, however harsh, the present business, then, perhaps, might come to a period. He consented to acknowledge, that he had acted wrong, but no farther. That was not enough. He now attempted to address Colonel King, who prevented him by saying, " That he was a d—d villain, and that he would not listen to any thing he had to say."

They proceeded. Colonel Fitzgerald's powder and balls were now expended. He desired to have one of King's pistols. To this I would not consent, though pressed to do so by my friends. Here ended this morning's business. We must meet again. It cannot end here. I have only to add, that nothing could exceed the firmness and propriety of Colonel King's conduct, through every stage of this business.

I am, my dear friend, very truly yours,
ROBERT WOOD.

P. S. On leaving the ground, Colonel

Fitzgerald agreed to meet Colonel King, at the same hour to morrow.

Both the Colonels, the same day, were put under arrest.

December 12, 1797.

Yesterday, intelligence was received in town of the death of Colonel Fitzgerald, who was lately guilty of a most shameful and dishonourable act in the family of the present Earl of Kingston, by seducing a daughter of that much respected nobleman, to whom he was allied, and in whose family he had been a constant visitor. He met with his death in the following manner:

After the discovery of this unfortunate criminal intercourse, which occurred in England, and in consequence of which, a duel had taken place between the brother of the young lady (who is now Lord Kingsborough) and the deceased Colonel Fitzgerald, she was removed to the country residence of her noble father, now the Earl of Kingston, at Mitchelstown, near Kilworth, in this kingdom. The deceased, feeling no remorse for what he had done, in dishonouring, by the most artful stratagems, an illustrious family, had the audacity and hardihood, to follow the young lady to Ireland; it is supposed, with a view to wrest her by violence from her parents: and, for this purpose, took lodgings at an inn in Kilworth.

The Colonel had been there some days, before his arrival at Kilworth was known, or the object of his expedition was discovered. He was observed to walk out in the night, and conceal himself in the day, and the servants, at length, noticed him lurking about Mitchelstown House, at unseasonable hours. Intelligence having reached Lord Kingsborough, who had had the duel with the Colonel; and, resolved to defeat his antagonist's project, he left his father's house, and went to Kilworth, where, having enquired if that gentleman was in the house, and being informed he was, he went to the apartment he was directed to, that the Colonel lodged in. Lord Kingsborough rapped at the door, requiring admittance. The Colonel, knowing his voice, replied, " that he was locked in, and could not open the door: but if he had any thing to say to him, he would receive it in writing under the door." This enraged the young nobleman, and he forced open the door, and running to a case of pistols in the room, took one, and desired the Colonel to take the other, and defend himself, as he was resolved to have satisfaction for the scheme the deceased had formed against his sister, and which he came to this place to put into execution. On both seizing the pistols, they grappled with each other, and were struggling, when the Earl of Kingston, who had been apprized of his son's departure in pursuit of the Colonel, and quickly followed the young lord, entered the room, and finding them in the contest, and that his son must lose his life, from the situation the deceased had him in, the Earl fired upon the Colonel, not, we believe, with an intention to kill him, though his aggravation was great. But the shot, however, took effect, and the Colonel lost his life, but not lamented by any one, who has heard of his very dishonourable conduct in this affair.

When Miss King was taken by her father from England, on account of her disgrace, it was discovered, on her arrival in Dublin, that the servant-maid, who accompanied her, favoured the views of the seducer. On her consequent dismissal from the service, she returned to England, and was the bearer of a private letter to Colonel Fitzgerald, the contents of which were, it is said, sufficient to induce the Colonel, even at the risk of his life, to make an effort to regain the young lady. But his finances not enabling him to undertake the journey, he borrowed a sum of money of an amiable woman, who ought to have been most dear to him, under the pretence of making a visit to Dorsetshire. Thus accommodated, he set out for the sister kingdom, and arrived at the village of Kilworth, near Mitchelstown, the residence of the noble family, the place where the young lady was then kept, and whose conduct was then watched with particular vigilance.

71.

Duel between the Right Hon. WILLIAM PITT *and* GEORGE TIERNEY, *Esq. May* 21, 1798.

IN consequence of some expressions made use of by Mr. Pitt, in the House of Commons, on Friday last, Mr. Pitt, accompanied by Mr. Rider, and Mr. Tierney, accompanied by Mr. George Walpole, met at three o'clock yesterday afternoon, on Putney Heath.

After some ineffectual attempts on the part of the seconds, to prevent farther proceedings, the parties took their ground, at the distance of twelve paces. A case of pistols was fired at the same moment, without effect. A second case was also fired, in the same manner. Mr. Pitt firing his pistol in the air, the seconds then jointly interfered, and insisted that the matter should go no farther, it being their decided opinion, that sufficient satisfaction had been given, and that the business was ended with perfect honour to both parties.

72.

Duel between Colonel HARVEY ASTON *and Major* ALLEN. *December 23, 1798.*

DIED at Madras, in consequence of a wound, which he received in a duel with Major Allen, of which he languished about a week, Colonel Harvey Aston.

He had been engaged in a similar affair of honour, and on the same account, with Major Picton, only the day preceding that on which he met Major Allen; but which was fortunately terminated by each party firing in the air, and a proper explanation taking place as to the offence.

73.

Duel between Messrs. COOLAN *and* MORCAN. *Dublin, March* 13, 1800.

THIS morning two students of our University, Messrs. Coolan and Morcan, in consequence of an unhappy dispute the preceding evening, met in the fields near Harcourt-street. They fired at the same moment, when Mr. Coolan's shot unfortunately took place in the temple of his antagonist, and killed him on the spot. The surviving combatant has been expelled the college, and the two seconds have been rusticated.

74.

Duel between JAMES CORRY, *Esq. and* —— NEWBURGH, *Esq.* *May* 10, 1800.

YESTERDAY a meeting took place on Drumcondra road, between James Corry, Esq., of Lurgan-street, and —— Newburgh, Esq. in consequence of a dispute, and, as alleged, the provocation of a blow given by the latter to the former. The latter gentleman was accompanied on the ground by Captain Warring, of the 24th Dragoons, as his second; the other by Mr. Weir, one of the attorneys.

Having taken their ground, the signal was given to fire. Mr. Corry's pistol went off without effect; Mr. Newburgh's missed fire. He was preparing to fire it afterwards, when his second called to him, telling him, the snap in duelling was considered as a fire. Both gentlemen were then provided with other pistols, and received the signal to fire again, which they did; and Mr. Newburgh was shot through the heart, and expired.

Mr. Newburgh was the only son of Broghill Newburgh, of the county of Cavan,

Esq., of an ancient family, and heir-apparent to an estate of £5,000. per annum.

Mr. Corry is an élève of the Speaker of the House of Commons, by whom he was placed in the lucrative situation of clerk to the Linen Board; a place which was enjoyed by his father, who was also a great favourite with Mr. Foster.

The deceased was upwards of thirty years of age, and married to the daughter of Mr. Camac, an East India gentleman, with a fortune of £30,000. He was related to Lord Enniskillen, Lord Erns, Lord Gosford, and some other of the best families in Ireland.

Mr. Corry, who is some years younger, is a young gentleman of amiable and inoffensive manners.

75.
Duel between Lieutenant B. and Mr. F., at Bombay. January 6, 1802.

A duel was fought, a few months since, at Bombay, between Lieutenant B. and a Mr. F., in which the latter was shot through the heart; and, of course, expired upon the spot.

The survivor and his second have both been sentenced to be transported to Botany Bay; the former for fourteen, the latter for seven years.

77.

Duel between Mr. P. HAMILTON *and Mr.* G. I. EAKER. *January,* 1802.

A duel took place at New York, between Mr. P. Hamilton, son of General Alexander Hamilton, and Mr. G. I. Eaker; in which, at the first fire, Mr. Hamilton was shot through the body. He languished until the next day, when he died.

77.

Duel between WILLIAM HUNTER, *Esq. and Mr.* DAVID MITCHELL. *August,* 1802.

AT Savannah, William Hunter, Esq. fell in a duel with Mr. David Mitchell.

The dispute had its origin in July last, in the county court, to the jury of which Mr. Hunter was foreman, in a cause in which Mitchell was counsel. During the trial, it appearing to Mr. Hunter that the examination of the evidence was not conducted by the counsel, with that impartiality which justice required, he addressed a few words to the court, when Mitchell got up and observed, " That Mr. Hunter was very officious on the occasion." Mr. Hunter replied, " That the officiousness of jurymen was not to be compared with the impertinence of some attorneys."

There the matter rested till August 9th, when Mitchell attacked Mr. Hunter in the street with a large bludgeon. Mr. Hunter having nothing to defend himself with, after receiving four blows, and attempting unsuccessfully, at the same time, to seize Mitchell by the collar, he said, " Mr. Mitchell, I am unarmed; I must retreat unless you lay aside your weapon." Mr. Hunter then retreated to Dr. Kollock's for a cane, but could not procure one. By this time some of the inhabitants interfered. The same evening Mr. Hunter sent Mr. Mitchell a challenge, who, after much equivocation, accepted it. Dr. Kollock was Mr. Hunter's second; Major B. Maxwell was second to Mitchell. Mr. Hunter fired first, and hit Mitchell on the hip; Mitchell missed Mr. Hunter. Mr. Hunter's second fire hit

Mitchell on the groin also, without penetrating the skin; but Mr. Hunter received Mitchell's second ball in his right breast. Mr. Hunter immediately turned, and exclaimed, "I am a dead man;" and as Drs. Glenn and Kollock caught him in their arms, he asked for a glass of wine, and expired.

78.

Duel between Lieutenant W., of the Navy, and Captain I., of the Army. March, 1803.

THIS morning a most extraordinary duel took place in Hyde-Park, between Lieutenant W., of the navy, and Captain I., of the army.

The antagonists arrived at the appointed place within a few minutes of each other. Some dispute arose respecting the distance, which the friends of Lieutenant W. insisted should not exceed six paces; while the seconds of Captain I. urged strongly the rashness of so decisive a distance, and insisted on its being extended. At length the proposal of Lieutenant W.'s friends was agreed to, and the parties fired per signal; when Lieutenant W. received the shot of his adversary on the guard of his pistol, which tore away the third and fourth fingers of his right hand. The seconds then interfered, to no purpose. The son of Neptune, apparently callous to pain, wrapped his handkerchief round his hand, and swore he had another, which never failed him. Captain I. called his friend aside, and told him it was in vain to urge a reconciliation. They again took their ground. On Lieutenant W. receiving the pistol in his left hand, he looked steadfastly at Captain I. for some time, then cast his eyes to heaven, and said, "Forgive me." The parties fired as before, and both fell. Captain I. received the shot through his head, and instantly expired. Lieutenant W. received the ball in his left breast, and immediately enquired of his friend if Captain I.'s wound was mortal? Being answered in the affirmative, he thanked heaven he had lived thus long. He requested that a mourning ring, which was on his finger, might be given to his sister; and that she might be assured, it was the happiest moment he ever knew. He had scarcely finished the word, when a quantity of blood burst from his wound, and he expired almost without a struggle.

The unfortunate young man was on the eve of being married to a lady in Hampshire, to whom, for some time, he had paid his addresses.

79.
Duel between Lieut-Colonel MONTGOMERY *and Captain* MACNAMARA. *April 6, 1803.*

THIS morning, as Lieut.-Colonel Montgomery and Captain Macnamara were riding in Hyde-Park, each followed by a Newfoundland dog, the dogs fought; in consequence of which, the gentlemen quarrelled, and used such irritating language to each other, that an exchange of address followed, and an appointment to meet at seven o'clock in the evening, near Primrose hill; the consequence of which proved fatal. Captain Macnamara's ball entered the right side of Colonel Montgomery's chest, and taking a direction to the left, most probably went through the heart; he instantly fell, without uttering a word, but rolled over two or three times, as if in great agony, and groaned. Colonel Montgomery's ball went through Captain Macnamara, entering on the right side, just above the hip, and passing through the left side, carrying part of the coat and waistcoat in with it, taking part of his leather breeches, and the hip button, away with it on the other side.

Colonel Montgomery was carried by some of the persons standing by, into Chalk-Farm, where he was laid on a bed, attended by Mr. Heaviside. As they were carrying him, he attempted to speak and spit; but the blood choaked him. His mouth foamed much; and in about five minutes after he was brought into the house, he expired with a gentle sigh.

Captain Macnamara is a naval officer, who has much distinguished himself in two or three actions, as commander in the Cerberus frigate. He lately returned from the West Indies; and his ship was, about two months ago, paid off at Chatham. He is about thirty-six years of age; a strong, bold, active man. He has fought two or three duels before; and was remarkable, at Cork, for keeping the turbulent in awe.

Colonel Montgomery was Lieutenant-Colonel of the Ninth Regiment of foot, son of Sir Robert Montgomery, of Ireland, and half-brother of Mrs. George Byng, and to the Marchioness of Townsend. He was a remarkably handsome man, and he had, also, fought bravely in the service of his country. In the Dutch expedition, the Russians being put to flight, his regiment was thrown into confusion, and retreated, in consequence of the Russians falling back upon them. At this time a drummer was killed, and Colonel Montgomery took up the drum, beating it to rally his men, he himself standing alone. He succeeded in rallying them, and at their head rendered essential service. On several occasions, in Egypt and Malta, he distinguished himself for his courage and spirit. He was very intimate with the Prince of Wales and Duke of York. The former shed tears on being apprized of the melancholy end of his friend.

April 15.

Yesterday morning, Mr. Heaviside, the surgeon, was arrested by Townsend, under authority of a warrant from Sir Richard Ford, wherein he stands charged with having been aiding and assisting in the murder of Colonel Montgomery : and, after undergoing a private examination, before the above magistrate, at Bow Street, he was fully committed to Newgate for trial, at the ensuing Old Bailey Sessions. Several witnesses were, also, privately examined respecting the duel, and bound over to appear on the trial.

Captain Macnamara was, yesterday, declared out of danger, but was not yet well enough to be removed.

The Coroner's inquest, on taking a view of the body of Colonel Montgomery, brought in a verdict of "Manslaughter." The remains were buried in a vault in St. James's Church.

Captain Macnamara was tried at the Old Bailey, and was led into court, supported by his friends, accompanied by Mr. Heaviside.

The evidence being closed, the prisoner addressed the jury in mitigation of his conduct.

Lords Hood, Nelson, Hotham, and Minto, and a great number of highly respectable gentlemen gave Captain Macnamara a most excellent character. Mr. Justice Heath summed up the evidence, and stated, that, from the pressure of the evidence, and the prisoner's own admission, the jury must find a verdict of "manslaughter." They were, however, of a different opinion; for, after retiring a quarter of an hour, they pronounced a verdict of " not guilty."

80.

Duel between LORD CAMELFORD *and Captain* BEST. *March*, 1804.

A duel has been fought between Lord Camelford and Captain Best, of the Royal Navy, in the fields behind Holland House, near Kensington.

The meeting is said to have taken place, in consequence of a quarrel between the parties, who were intimate friends, on the preceding evening, at the Prince of Wales's Coffee House.

About half-past eight o'clock, the parties and their seconds, arrived, two on horseback, and two in a post-chaise, opposite to

Holland House, and were observed to pass over into the fields. In a short time, the firing of pistols was heard, and when a labourer, who was working in an adjoining garden, repaired to the spot, he found Lord Camelford lying on his back, in the lower part of the field, which was overflowed, to the depth of several inches in water. Captain Best and his friend, had rode off, directly after the shot took effect, and the other gentleman followed their example, immediately on the countryman's coming up, on the pretence of going for a surgeon.

His lordship was unwilling to be removed, and it was, with difficulty, that those, who came to his assistance, got him placed in a chair, and conveyed to Mr. Ottey's, at Little Holland House. His adversary's ball had penetrated his right shoulder. When questioned as to the names of the other gentlemen who had accompanied him, he declined giving any satisfaction on the subject.

He was attended in the course of the day, by Mr. Heaviside, Mr. Thomson and Mr. Horne, surgeons. A Mr. Nihell, or Nield, we understand, was second to Captain Best, and the Hon. Mr. Devereux was second to Lord Camelford.

March, 12.

On Saturday evening, this unfortunate nobleman breathed his last. He sent for his Solicitor, Mr. Wilson, of Lincoln's Inn Fields, and made his will the night after the accident; and he maintained the most perfect composure under his sufferings to the last.

We are authorized to say, that Lord Camelford has left behind him a paper, in his own hand-writing, fully acquitting his antagonist from any blame, in the late unfortunate transaction.

In the voluminous evidence, adduced before the Coroner's inquest, it was proved, that Lord Camelford had declared, " That he was the aggressor, that he forgave the gentleman who had shot him, and that he hoped God would forgive him too."

Mr. Hodgson, the Coroner, in his address to the jury, made the following observations:

" It was evident the deceased had been killed by a shot fired at him by some person, of whose identity the jury had no direct or admissible proof. The laws of this country admitted of no excuse for one man killing another in a private duel. But, supposing the person, who had slain the deceased, to be able, before a superior tribunal, to offer circumstances and facts, in palliation of his offence, they could not have any weight in this inquest. He had, strictly speaking, been guilty of murder, and to that effect must necessarily be the verdict of the the jury. In the present case, there was no doubt of the deceased having been feloniously killed. But, there was no evidence who was the principal; or, who were the seconds. In point of fact they were all equally guilty: for, in the crime of murder, accessories before the fact, were considered as principals. There was hardly a doubt, that the expressions and avowal, of the deceased, so honourably made in favour of his opponent, would, if the latter were arraigned in a superior court, induce his acquittal. But that was a consideration, which ought not to operate on the minds of those, whom he was addressing. Had the parties been in a room, and upon a sudden quarrel, the deceased, having given the first provocation, had been killed, it might have been justifiable homicide. But, on the contrary, it appeared, they had deliberately gone out to commit an unjustifiable act. Had it been proved, who the person was, who fired the shot at the deceased, the jury would have been bound to have returned an identical charge of " murder" against him, and those, who were aiding and abetting him. But, as the case stood, they would only pronounce the verdict, to which he had alluded.

The jury, unanimously, returned a verdict of "wilful murder,"or "felonious homicide," " by some person, or persons, unknown."

81.

Duel between the Hon. Aaron Burr *and General* A. Hamilton. *August,* 1804.

The American papers have brought an account of a melancholy affair of honour, between the Hon. Aaron Burr, (Vice President of the United States) and General A. Hamilton, who was appointed to succeed Mr. Livingstone, Ambassador at Paris.

The origin of the dispute was, from a pamphlet published by Dr. Cooper, in which is the following passage: " General Hamilton and Dr. Kent say, that they consider Colonel Burr as a dangerous man, and one unfit to be trusted with the reins of government." In another place Dr. Cooper says, " General Hamilton has expressed of Mr. Burr, opinions still more despicable." This latter passage excited the resentment of Colonel Burr, who sent his friend with a letter to General Hamilton, in which he demands "a prompt and unqualified acknowledgment, or denial, of the expression, which could justify this inference on the part of Dr. Cooper."

General Hamilton, in his answer, admits the first statement, " the language of which," he contends, " comes fairly within the bounds prescribed in cases of political animosity." He objects to Colonel Burr's demand, by considering it as "too indefinite," or, " as calling on him, to retrace every conversation, which he had held, either publicly, or confidentially, in the course of fifteen years opposition; and, to contradict that, which, very possibly, had escaped his memory. If any thing more definite, should be proposed, he expressed his willingness to give Colonel Burr all due satisfaction."

Colonel Burr, in his reply, insists upon a general retractation, and says, "It is no matter to him, whether his honour has been attacked loudly or in whispers." General Hamilton rejoins, by calling for something more defined, and refuses either a general denial, or a general acknowledgment. The meeting was, then, demanded by Colonel Burr.

Previous to repairing to the ground, the General drew up his will, and inclosed in it a paper, containing his reflections on the meeting. He says, "On my expected interview with Colonel Burr, I think proper to make some remarks, explanatory of my conduct, motives, and views. I was certainly desirous of avoiding this interview, for the most cogents.

1.—My religious and moral principles are strongly opposed to the practice of duelling: and it would ever give me pain to be obliged to shed the blood of a fellow creature in a private combat, forbidden by the laws.

2.—My wife and children are extremely dear to me; and my life is of the utmost importance to them, in various views.

3.—I feel a sense of obligation towards my creditors, who, in case of accident to me, by the forced sale of my property, may be in some degree, sufferers. I did not think myself at liberty, as a man of probity, lightly to expose them to hazard.

4.—I am conscious of no ill-will to Colonel Burr, distinct from political opposition, which, as I trust, has proceeded from pure and upright motives.

Lastly.—I shall hazard much, and can possibly gain nothing by the issue of the interview."

It also appears that General Hamilton had determined not to return Colonel Burr's fire: but, that, on his receiving the shock of a mortal wound, his pistol went off involuntarily, and without being aimed at Colonel Burr. This statement, being denied by the opposite party, search for the ball was made, and it was found lodged in a cedar tree, at the height of eleven feet and a half, fourteen paces from the place where General Hamilton stood, and more than four feet out of the line of direction between the parties. When the General fell, Colonel Burr walked towards him, with apparent gestures of regret. But he did not speak to him, as he was hurried from the ground by his friends.

The funeral of the General was observed at New York, with unusual respect and ceremony. All the public functionaries attended. All the bells in the city were muffled, and tolled during the day. The shops, at the instance of the Common Council, were shut, all business suspended, and the principal inhabitants engaged to wear mourning for six weeks.

After the funeral service, Mr. Morris, the Governor of New York, on a stage erected in the Portico of Trinity Church, having four of General Hamilton's sons, the eldest about sixteen, and the youngest about six years of age, with him, delivered to an immense concourse in front, an extemporary funeral oration, expressive of the merits of the deceased, and of the loss, which America has sustained in his death.

The New York Advertiser says—That no death, since that of "the Great and Good Washington," has filled the Republic with such deep and universal regret.

The coroner's inquest, held on the body of General Hamilton, have brought in a verdict of "wilful murder," against Aaron Burr, Esq. Vice President of the United States, and against W. P. Van Ness, Esq. Attorney, and N. Pendleton, Esq. Counsellor, as accessaries.

82.

Duel between Ensign BROWNE *and Lieutenant* BUTLER.   *January* 1, 1806.

THIS morning, a meeting took place in a piece of ground, in the parish of Basford, between Ensign Browne, of the 36th Regiment of foot, and Lieutenant Butler, of the 83d Regiment, on the recruiting service, at Nottingham.

The parties fired together by signal, when, unfortunately, Ensign Browne was shot through the heart, and instantly expired, without uttering a word.

Lieutenant Butler and the seconds immediately withdrew. The body of the deceased was taken to Basford church, by some persons who were attracted to the spot by the report of the pistols: and a verdict of "wilful murder" was returned by the Coroner's jury who sate upon it.

Ensign Browne was a promising young officer, of a very respectable family in Ireland, and had only just attained his seventeenth year. He and Lieutenant Butler belonged, lately, to the same regiment: but from a serious disagreement which took place between them, the Commander-in-Chief ordered them to be placed in different corps. On their meeting at Nottingham, however, the embers of animosity rekindled, and the unhappy result has proved the loss to society of a valuable and much respected young member.

83.

Duel between MAJOR BROOKES *and Colonel* BOLTON. *January* 4, 1806.

ABOUT a year ago, a duel was to have taken place at Liverpool, between Major Brookes and Colonel Bolton, in consequence of a quarrel. But the affair being known, they were bound to keep the peace, for one year. After this, the animosity between them increased daily, and each reproached the other, with having informed the officers of justice of their intention to fight.

The time, for which they were bound to keep the peace elapsed on Friday week, when a challenge passed, and an immediate meeting was determined upon. They met, and at the first fire Major Brookes was killed on the spot. The Colonel absconded.

84.

Duel between Lieutenant TURRENS *and Mr.* FISHER. *March* 22, 1806.

A duel was fought on Galleywood Common, near Chelmsford, Essex, between Lieutenant Turrens and Mr. Fisher, both of the Sixth Regiment of foot, in barracks there. The parties, with their seconds, arrived on the spot, appointed for the encounter, at day-break, when the preliminaries having been settled, they took a short distance, and turning round, fired at the same instant. The Lieutenant received his antagonist's ball in the groin, and immediately fell. On which Mr. Fisher went up, and took him by the hand, expressing much regret at the lamentable consequence that had ensued, as, from the nature of the wound, he was apprehensive it would prove mortal.

Assistance having been procured, the wounded gentleman was removed to a windmill, at a short distance, and as soon as possible, conveyed from thence to his apartments in the barracks, where every attention was rendered, that his unfortunate situation could require. The ball having lodged on the side opposite to which it entered, was extracted by Dr. Welch, at four o'clock the same afternoon, but he expired between nine and ten o'clock, on Sunday morning. An inquisition was taken by J. O. Parker, Jun. Esq. Coroner, on view of the body, on Monday, and a verdict returned of " wilful murder," against Mr. Fisher, and the two seconds ; one of whom is under arrest. Mr. Fisher and the other have absconded.

85.

Duel between Baron HOMPESCH *and Mr.* RICHARDSON. *Sept.* 22, 1806.

A duel was fought this morning, between Baron Hompesch and a Mr. Richardson, of Colchester, in consequence of the Baron, who is near-sighted, running against Mr. Richardson and two ladies, in the street. On the exchange of the third pistol, Mr. Richardson was shot through the body.

86.

Duel between Mr. ROGERS *and Mr.* LONG. *Dublin, May* 3, 1806.

THIS day a duel was fought in Foster Avenue, between two young gentlemen, of the Barrack-office, in this city, and intimate friends, upon occasion of a tavern quarrel, the preceding evening.

On the first fire, at the distance of eleven paces, both parties fell; the one, Mr. Rogers, received a ball through his heart, and of course died instantly. The other, Mr. Long, was shot through both his thighs, and is also since dead.

87.

Duel between Sir FRANCIS BURDETT *and Mr.* PAULL. *May* 5, 1807.

ON account of a misunderstanding between Sir Francis Burdett and Mr. Paull, a meeting took place at nine o'clock this morning, near Wimbledon Common. Mr. Paull conceiving his character very injuriously reflected upon by Sir Francis, dispatched a challenge, late on Friday night, to the Baronet; which being accepted, the parties met early yesterday morning at Combe Wood, near Wimbledon Common.

They discharged two pistols each. The second shot, fired by Mr. Paull, wounded Sir Francis in the thigh; the second pistol, fired by Sir Francis, wounded Mr. Paull in the leg. Sir Francis returned home in the same carriage with Mr. Paull.

The account of the duel between Sir Francis Burdett and Mr. Paull, signed by Sir Francis's second.

ON Saturday morning, May 5th, about half past five o'clock, Sir Francis Burdett's servant came to me with a note from Sir Francis, desiring me to come to him instantly to Wimbledon, with a pair of pistols, as he had been called upon; but did not say by whom. I could procure none, after trying at two officers of the Guards; and at Manton's, but found none fit for the purpose. It occurring to me that going thus from place to place for pistols, might at last be the occasion of bringing on more notice than I wished, I determined to proceed without them, thinking that those who called upon him must have a pair at least; and that if it was necessary, they might serve both parties. I arrived at Sir Francis Burdett's house, at Wimbledon, about eight o'clock, having been obliged to wait more than two hours for a chaise. He was gone on to the King's Arms, Kingston, having left a note for me to follow him there in his carriage. On entering Kingston, I saw Mr. Paull in a coach, accompanied by another person, and a servant on the coach seat. He called out to me on passing his carriage, and said something that I did not distinctly hear; but I think he advised me not to proceed into the town, as the affair would be blown. I asked him where the inn was, and went on.

As soon as I entered the room where Burdett was sitting, a person appeared, who had followed me. On his entrance I asked Burdett who he was? He said, it was Paull's second. I then said, "Whom have I the honour to address?" "My name is Cooper." "Do you know him, Burdett?" "I have no doubt Mr. Paull has appointed a proper person to meet me." "Sir, sir, sir," was Mr. Cooper's answer. I then said, as Burdett desired, that we should immediately follow them, if they proceeded to Combe Wood, which seemed to be a proper place for meeting.

After Burdett had given me some letters and memorandums, for different friends, and explained to me the subject of Mr. Paull's demands, we proceeded to the place appointed; where, ordering the carriages to stop for us, we went into the wood to a considerable distance. I fixed on a proper spot. During our walk, Mr. Paull frequently addressed me on the subject of the quarrel. He said, he was sure I had not heard it rightly stated, and wished me much to hear him. I always replied, that I had heard the whole from my principal, and that I placed implicit confidence in what he said; for if I could not have done that, I should not have accompanied him there; and, that from all I heard and read concerning the matter, it was my decided opinion, that Burdett was the person most entitled to consider himself as ill-used: but that, at all events, an apology from him was out of all question, and that I would rather see him shot, than advise him to so disgraceful an act. As Mr. Paull did not seem to have at all placed his opinions, or case, in the hands of his second, I found it in vain to talk to him on the subject of an accommodation. After we had stopped, I asked for the pistols, which were produced by Mr. Cooper, who declared that he had not expected things would have taken this turn. I asked him, if he expected I should advise, or Burdett would consent, to disgrace himself. I then told him, we had been unable to obtain pistols, and expected he would consent, as well as Mr. Paull, that we should use one of theirs. To this they both agreed. He, Mr. Cooper, told me he did not know how to load them; I shewed him how, and directed him to load Burdett's, while I loaded Mr. Paull's. I then asked him, what distance he proposed them to stand at; he said he knew nothing about the matter, and left it to me. I measured out twelve paces, and placed the principals at the extremity of the space. I then directed him to give Sir Francis a pistol, and I presented another to Mr. Paull; at the same time assuring him, as I had Mr. Cooper, that Sir Francis came there without the slightest animosity against Mr. Paull; but that he would fire at him, as a mode of self-defence. I said besides to Mr. Paull, "That I hoped he was thoroughly convinced, that the injury he had received, was of a nature not to be satisfied with any thing, short of attempting the life of my friend, and risking his own." He replied, " He must do so, unless he had an apology."

I then asked them, if they would agree to fire by a signal I would make by dropping my handkerchief? They each did agree to it. I placed myself about four yards on one side the centre of the space between them; while Mr. Cooper, on giving the pistol to Sir Francis, retreated very precipitately behind a tree at some distance. On a signal being made, they fired together, but without effect. I then took Mr. Paull's pistol from him, and said, " I hope, Sir, you are now satisfied." He said, " No; he must have an apology, or proceed." I said, " To talk of an apology was absurd, and quite out of all question." I then reloaded the pistols, and gave them as before. I again addressed Mr. Paull as I had at first. He answered with warmth, " That he must have an apology, or proceed;" and called God to witness that he was the most injured man on earth. Mr. Cooper was then to make the signal; but he stood so far out of the way, that Sir Francis could not see him, although he had already called to him during his retreat, and begged him not to go so far off, and to come forwards, or words to that effect. At last, I saw Sir Francis could not see Mr. Cooper, nor his signal; and upon his making it, I called out, " Fire," to Sir Fancis, as soon as I saw Mr. Paull raise his pistol. They did so together, I believe upon my uttering the words.

I should observe, that while they were

waiting for the signal, I observed that Sir Francis held his arm raised, and his pistol pointed towards Mr. Paull. Knowing this was not with a view of taking any unfair advantage, but the effect of accident, I said, " Burdett, don't take aim. I am sure you are not doing so, drop your arm, as you see Mr. Paull has his pistol pointed downwards." Mr. Paull then asked me, " why I advised Sir Francis not to take aim?" I said, "any body might see that I could only mean for him not to take aim, or prepare to do so, before the signal, and from a desire to see, that they were upon equal terms." The consequences of the second shots have been already described. After speaking to each of them, I set off for the carriages. Both were put into Mr. Paull's. I went on to Sir Francis Burdett's house, to Lady Burdett and his brother; and also to procure a surgeon at Wimbledon.

During the transaction not one word passed between me and Sir Francis, except what I said about taking aim. Mr. Cooper has constantly refused to sign any official account, to say where he lives, or what is his situation; which also was repeatedly requested of him before me; nor do I at this moment know any thing further about him.

JOHN BELLENDEN KER.

88.

Duel between Lieutenants T. *and* R. *Extract of a Letter, dated New Orleans, October* 1, 1807.

"THIS morning, at ten o'clock, I shook Lieutenant T. by the hand; and this evening, at eight, I held in my hand a ball that had passed through his heart. The best account I can give you of this melancholy affair is this:

"A number of officers were amusing themselves in their quarters, last evening, with cards, when R. came in, and was asked to play; he declined, with a quotation from Shakspeare. Some criticism was made on it by T., and an argument of some warmth took place. Disagreeable reflections were made, bad language ensued, and this morning T. sent R. a challenge. They met just before night, opposite to this city. On the word, " Fire," T.'s pistol flashed, and R.'s snapped; on the second, they both fired almost at the same instant, and R.'s ball passed quite through T.'s body, and lodged in the left sleeve of his shirt; he staggered a few paces, exclaimed, " I'm a dead man," fell into the arms of his friend, and instantly expired. What a dreadful affair is this! And how much is to be lamented the frequency of such occurrences! R. did not wish to fight him; but unfortunately, all attempts at accommodation were vain; T., poor fellow, would listen to no proposals. He had a strong presentiment of his fate, and expressed it; but he behaved with the utmost firmness and resolution. R. was much affected, and embraced him in the agonies of death, exclaiming, in a frantic manner, ' My dear friend, why would you force me to do this? Let me declare in your dying ear, that I have no enmity to you; that I did not wish to meet you; and that I shall mourn your death as that of a brother.' "

89.

Duel between Mr. ARTHUR SMITH *and Mr.* THOMAS HUSTON. *April,* 1808.

AT Beaufort, in South Carolina, died in the evening, Mr. Arthur Smith; and the next morning, Mr. Thomas Huston. In the morning these young men arose in all the vigour of health; in a few hours both were bleeding on the field of honour. A challenge had been given, and accepted. A duel was fought, and both were mortally wounded.

90.

Duel between Major CAMPBELL *and Captain* BOYD. *August,* 1808.

Ireland. Armagh Assizes.

Trial of Major CAMPBELL, *of the* 21*st. Regiment.*

ALEXANDER CAMPBELL, Brevet-Major in the army, and a Captain in the 21st Regiment, stood indicted for the "wilful and felonious murder" of Alexander Boyd, a captain in the said regiment, by shooting him, the said Alexander Boyd, with a pistol bullet.

To support this indictment, the following witnesses were produced.

George Adams, who stated, that he had been assistant surgeon in the 21st Regiment, since April, twelvemonths. He knew Major Campbell and Captain Boyd. In the year 1807, they were quartered in the barracks, in the county of Armagh, side of Newry. On the 23rd of the said month, Captain Boyd died of a wound he received by a pistol bullet, which penetrated the extremity of the four false ribs, and lodged in the cavity of the belly. On that day, the regiment was inspected by General Kerr; and, after the inspection, the General and officers messed together. About eight o'clock, all the officers left the mess, except Major Campbell, Captain Boyd, witness, and a Lieutenant Hall. A conversation then commenced by Major Campbell stating, "That General Kerr corrected him, that day, about a particular mode of giving a word of command, when he conceived he gave it right." He mentioned how he gave it, and how the General had corrected him. Captain Boyd remarked, " that neither was correct according to Dundas, which was the King's order." (This observation, witness stated, was made in the usual mode of conversation.) Major Campbell said, " it might not be according to the King's order, but still he conceived it was not incorrect." Captain Boyd still insisted " it was not correct, according to the King's order." They argued this some time, till Captain Boyd said, " he knew it as well as any man." Major Campbell replied, "he doubted that much." Captain Boyd at length said, " he knew it better than he, let him take that as he liked." Major Campbell then got up and said, " Then, Captain Boyd, do you say, that I am wrong ?" Captain Boyd replied, " I do. I know I am right by the King's orders." Major Campbell then quitted the room. Captain Boyd remained after him for some time. He left the room before the witness or Lieutenant Hall. But no observation was made on his going, more than any other gentleman that had dined there. The witness and Lieutenant Hall went out together in a short time after. They went to a second mess room, and there Captain Boyd came and spoke to them. (The conversation was not admitted, as Major Campbell was not present at it.) They then went out together, and the witness left Captain Boyd at Lieutenant Dewars's. In about twenty minutes after he was called upon to visit Captain Boyd. He went, and found him on a chair vomiting. He examined his wound, and found it a very dangerous one. He survived it but eighteen hours. He staid with him till he died, during which time he got gradually worse till his dissolution.

On his cross examination, he stated, that there was something irritating in Captain Boyd's manner of making the observation alluded to; so much so, that he conceives Major Campbell could not, consistent with his feelings, pass it over. But, if a candid explanation had taken place, he did not conceive the melancholy affair would have occurred.

John Hoey stated, That he is mess-waiter for the 21st regiment, and was so then. He remembers the night this affair took place. Knew Major Campbell and Captain Boyd. He saw Major Campbell that

Q

night in a room where he was washing glasses. Major Campbell had quitted the room ten or fifteen minutes. As Major Campbell was coming up stairs, Captain Boyd was leaving the mess-room, and they met on the stair-head. Both went into the mess-waiter's room, and there remained ten or fifteen minutes, when they separated. The prisoner, in about twenty minutes, came again to the witness, and desired him to go to Captain Boyd, and tell him a gentleman wished to speak to him, if he pleased. He accordingly went in search of Captain Boyd. He found him on the parade ground. He delivered the message, and Captain Boyd accompanied him to the mess-room. No one was there. The witness pointed to a little room off it, as the room the gentleman was in. He then went to the mess-kitchen, and in eight or ten minutes he heard the report of a shot: thought nothing of it till he heard another. He then went to the mess-room, and there saw Captain Boyd and Lieutenants Hall and Macpherson. Captain Boyd was sitting on a chair vomiting. Major Campbell was gone, but in about ten or twelve minutes he came to the room where the witness was washing some glasses. Major Campbell asked for candles. He got a pair, and brought them into the small room. Major Campbell shewed the witness the corners of the room, in which each person stood, which distance measured seven paces. He never saw Major Campbell after, till a week ago, though the witness never quitted the regiment, and retained his employment.

John Macpherson stated, That he is Lieutenant in the said regiment. Knew Major Campbell and Captain Boyd. Recollects the day of the duel. On the evening of that day, going up stairs about nine o'clock, he heard, as he thought, Major Campbell say, " On the word of a dying man, is every thing fair ?" He got up before Captaid Boyd replied : he said, " Campbell, you have hurried me, you're a bad man." Witness was in coloured clothes, and Major Campbell did not know him, but said again, " Boyd, before this stranger and Lieutenant Hall, was every thing fair ?" Captain Boyd replied, " O my Campbell, you know I wanted you to wait, and have friends." Major Campbell then said, " Good God, will you mention before these gentlemen, was not every thing fair? Did not you say, you were ready?" Captain Boyd answered, "Yes," but, in a moment after, said, "Campbell, you are a bad man." Captain Boyd was helped into the next room, and Major Campbell followed, much agitated, and repeatedly said to Captain Boyd, "that he (Boyd) was the happiest man of the two." "I am (said Major Campbell) an unfortunate man, but I hope not a bad one." Major Campbell asked Captain Boyd if he forgave him? He stretched out his hand, and said, "I forgive you, I feel for you, and I am sure you do for me." Major Campbell then left the room.

Duncan Dewar, Adjutant of the regiment, who was with Captain Boyd for some time after he was wounded, was produced to shew Captain Boyd's firm conviction he would die in consequence of that wound, in order to let in his declaration then made as evidence. But Captain Boyd not having (before him) expressed such a conviction, that evidence failed. Surgeon W. J. Nice, was produced to the same point, and likewise failed.

Colonel Paterson of the 21st regiment, was produced to the same point, and also failed.

George Sutherland, Quarter-master of the same regiment, was produced to the same point. He stated that he saw him ten minutes before he died. He was in bed, agitated with pain, in his senses, but rolling in the bed. He did not, however, say to him, that he thought he was dying.

Upon this, a special verdict was directed to the jury, to enquire whether Captain Boyd, ten minutes before his death, and under the circumstances stated, must or must not, have known he was dying. After some short deliberation, they found for the affirmative of this issue (that he must have known it). The declaration was then admitted, but none could be proved within that place, except his asking for Major Campbell, and his saying, " Poor man, I am sorry for him."

John Greenhill was produced merely to prove, that Major Campbell had time to cool after the altercation took place; inasmuch as he went home, drank tea with his family, and gave him a box to leave with Lieutenant Hall, before the affair took place.

Here the prosecution closed.

The defence set up, was merely and exclusively as to the character of the prisoner, for humanity, peaceable conduct, and proper behaviour. To this, several officers of the highest rank were produced, who vouched for it to the fullest extent, namely, Colonel Paterson, of the 21st regiment, General Campbell, General Graham Sterling, Captain Macpherson, Captain Menzies, Colonel Grey, and many others, whom it was unnecessary to produce.

The learned Judge charged the jury in the most able manner; recapitulated the evidence, and explained the law on the subject, most fully and clearly. The jury retired, and in about half an hour brought in a verdict, " Guilty of murder;" but recommended him to mercy, on the score of character only.

He was sentenced to be executed on Monday, but respited to Wednesday sen'-night.

August 25.

THIS unfortunate officer suffered at twelve o'clock at noon, on Wednesday week, amidst a vast multitude of spectators. He met his fate with pious and becoming fortitude, having spent his last moments with Dr. Bowie, the father of his amiable and distressed widow. His body, after having been suspended the usual time, was put into a hearse in waiting, which left the town immediately, escorted by Dr. Bowie, for Ayr, in Scotland, to be interred in the family vault. To describe the distresses of the fond widow of the deceased, would be impossible. Mrs. Campbell, who, it is already known, has used every effort to preserve the life of her partner, left London by the Glasgow mail, on Saturday night, frantic betwixt hope and despair; but still cheered with the probability of her solicitude obtaining, at least, another respite. On Monday morning, the friend of her husband, at whose house in Bury-street, St. James's, she resided, whilst in London, received a letter from the lady's father, with the intelligence, " That Major Campbell was no more." Mrs. Campbell reached

Ayr on Tuesday morning, the very time the corpse of her husband arrived;—and we must here close the tragic scene!

Major Campbell, in his conversation with his intimate friends, previously to surrendering himself, had always said, that if he were convicted of murder, he should suffer, as an example to duellists in Ireland; but it was always his opinion, that a jury would not convict him of murder.

It has been erroneously stated, that the jury recommended the deceased, merely from his universal good character; but the jury recommended him in consequence of the duel having been a fair one; although, by the direction of the Judge, they were bound, on their oaths, to convict the prisoner of murder. Major Campbell, previous to his death, observed, that life was not an object so dear to him, as the reflection was distressing, that his children and family should bear the stigma, that he was executed for murder.

The fate of this unfortunate gentleman has been rendered peculiarly interesting, by the unremitting exertions of Mrs. Campbell to procure a mitigation of his punishment;

in the prosecution of which, she appears to have endured fatigues of body and mind, which might be supposed too great for female strength. On her arrival at Windsor, with a memorial to His Majesty, supplicating mercy, it was past eight o'clock, and His Majesty had retired to his apartment. Her Majesty, notwithstanding, presented the memorial that night; and Mrs. Campbell received the kindest attention from the whole of the Royal Family. But it appears to have been a case, to which the Royal mercy could not be extended; and the law has been, accordingly, permitted to take its course.

Major Campbell made his escape from Ireland after the duel, and lived with his family, under a fictitious name, for several months, at Chelsea. The duel took place in June, 1807; but his mind became so uneasy, that he at last determined to surrender himself, be the result what it might.

He was first cousin of the Earl of Breadalbane, a man esteemed and beloved by all his friends. It is superfluous to add, that

Mrs. Campbell is a most amiable woman. She has four infant children.

The unfortunate catastrophe, which produced such an awful result to Major Campbell, it is hoped, will not fail to leave a lesson to mankind of salutary influence. Both of the parties were gentlemen, eminent in their profession, of high character and honour, who had long lived on terms of mutual friendship and esteem. The unfortunate irritation of a moment, at once deprived society of one of the best of men, and left a widow and infant family to mourn their irreparable loss. Retribution of the most awful kind has fallen to the lot of the other; and his amiable widow and helpless family, are also involved in all the distress which the human mind can conceive.

From the period of the unhappy event, to the closing of the tragic scene, Major Campbell evinced the most heartfelt grief for what had happened to his friend.

91.

Duel between Lord PAGET *and the Hon. Captain* CADOGAN. *May*, 1809.

IN order to prevent the appearance in the papers of any mis-statement respecting the duel, which took place this morning, between Lord Paget and Captain Cadogan, We, the respective friends of the parties, feel it incumbent on us to submit the following, as the correct statement of the event, as it occurred.

In consequence of a challenge having been received by Lord Paget from Captain Cadogan, and every attempt to prevent a meeting having failed, the parties, attended by their respective friends; Captain Cadogan by Captain Mackenzie, of the navy; Lord Paget by Lieut. Colonel Vivian, of the 7th Light Dragoons; met, as agreed, at seven o'clock, on Wimbledon common. The ground having been taken at twelve paces distance, they were directed to fire together. Captain Cadogan fired: Lord Paget's pistol flashed. This having been decided to go for a fire, a question arose, whether Lord Paget had taken aim, as if intending to hit his antagonist. Both the seconds being clearly of opinion that such was not his intention (although the degree of obliquity he gave the direction of the pistol was such as to have been discovered only by particular observation), Captain Mackenzie stated to Captain Cadogan, that as it appeared to be Lord Paget's intention not to fire at him, he could not admit of the affair proceeding any farther. Lieut. Colonel Vivian then asked Captain Cadogan, whether he had not himself observed, that Lord Paget had not aimed at him. To which he replied in the affirmative. Captain Mackenzie then declared his determination not to remain any longer in the field, to witness any further act of hostility on the part of Captain Cadogan. Captain Cadogan replied, that of course his conduct must be decided by his second; declaring, at the same time, that he had come prepared for the fall of one of the parties. On Captain Mackenzie and Lieut. Colonel Vivian making it known to Lord Paget, that as he evidently did not intend to fire at Captain Cadogan, the affair could go no farther; his Lordship replied, " As such is your determination, I have now no hesitation in saying, that nothing could ever have induced me to add to the injuries I have already done the family, by firing at the brother of Lady Charlotte Wellesley." The parties then left the ground.

(*Signed*) R. H. VIVIAN.
           GEORGE CHARLES MACKENZIE.

The cause of the above duel is well known. It arose from the seduction of the lady of the Honourable Henry Wellesley (sister of Captain Cadogan) by Lord Paget. Her husband afterwards gained £20,000. damages in the Sheriff's Court.

92.

Duel between LORD CASTLEREAGH *and Mr.* CANNING.   *Sept.* 21, 1809.

A duel took place early this morning, between Lord Castlereagh and Mr. Canning, in which the latter received a wound in the left thigh; but happily it is not dangerous, being merely a flesh wound.

The meeting took place at Putney Heath.

Lord Yarmouth seconded Lord Castlereagh, and Mr. R. Ellis accompanied Mr. Canning. We understand they fired by signal, at the distance of ten yards. The first missed; and no explanation taking place, they fired a second time, when Mr. Canning was wounded in the left thigh, on the outer side of the bone: and thus the affair terminated. He was put into a coach, and conveyed to Gloucester Lodge, his newly purchased seat at Brompton, and Lord Castlereagh returned to his house in St. James's Square.

93.

Duel between Mr. GEORGE PAYNE *and Mr.* CLARK. *September* 6, 1810.

A fatal duel was fought on Thursday morning upon Wimbledon Common, by two gentlemen.

At half-past five o'clock, three post chaises were noticed passing over Putney Bridge, and at half-past six, one of the chaises returned to the Red Lion, at Putney, with a wounded gentleman, of the name of Payne. Mr. Heaviside was sent for, and found that a pistol ball had gone through the groin. The unfortunate gentleman died at half-past four o'clock on Thursday afternoon.

Mr. George Payne was the younger son of the late Renè Payne, Esq. and he left him his fortune, to the amount of £14,000. per annum. In that settlement, the whole now goes to his eldest son, except £500. a year to his widow, and £10,000. to his younger children. Mr. Payne has left four children by his wife, who was a Miss Gray.

The cause of the fatal duel is truly melancholy. The challenge took place about ten days ago, at Scarborough, but the quarrel was of a more distant date. The orphan daughter of the late Dr. Clark, of Newcastle, was the friend of Mrs. Payne, and a visitor in the family. An unfortunate attachment took place between Mr. Payne and Miss Clark, which, transpiring, the irritated feelings of the brother forced him to resent. Every means were tried by Mr. John Payne, the elder brother of the deceased, to avert the catastrophe, but in vain.

Mr. George Payne was most exemplary in all his conduct through life, except in this fatal attachment. He was a most liberal and most amiable man. He had whispered to his second, Mr. Abbott, that he should not return Mr. Clark's fire; but the first shot was mortal. Mr. Clark has effected his escape.

94.

Duel between Captain BOARDMAN *and Ensign* DE BETTON. *March* 4, 1811.

IN consequence of a trifling quarrel, a duel took place at Barbadoes, on the 15th of January, between Captain Boardman, of the second battalion of the 60th regiment, and Ensign De Betton, of the Royal West India Rangers, in which, at the first fire, the former was shot through the heart, and instantly expired. The survivor immediately escaped from the island.

95.

Duel between Mr. HARRISON *and* ———.
May 9, 1811.

A duel was fought, on Tuesday morning, at day-break, in a field, about a mile and a half from Totteridge, between two gentlemen, who had alighted from post chaises, at the King's Arms public house, near the spot. In an hour after, one of the parties was brought in, mortally wounded in the abdomen, and he died in four hours after. A jury was held, and the fact of the duel being proved by some husbandmen, a verdict of " wilful murder," was returned. The body was owned after the inquest. The deceased was a Mr. Harrison, a young man about twenty-two years of age.

96.

Duel between Lieut. BLUNDELL, 101*st Regiment, and Mr.* MAGUIRE, 6*th West India Regiment. July* 12, 1813.

A duel was fought, yesterday, at Carisbrook Castle, Isle of Wight, at half-past 2 o'clock,

R

p. m. (*agreeably to the written challenge of Lieut. Blundell,*) between that gentleman and Mr. Maguire, when at the second discharge of pistols, Mr. B. received a mortal wound, of which he died two days after.

97.

Duel between Lieutenant STEWART *and Lieutenant* BAGNALL. *October* 7, 1812.

A fatal duel took place on South Sea Common, near Portsmouth. The parties were, Lieutenant Stewart and Lieutenant Bagnall, of the Royal Marines, and most intimate friends. The quarrel arose concerning a female, with whom both were intimate.

In the first case of pistols, Lieutenant Stewart's missed fire. In the second discharge, his ball entered behind Lieutenant Bagnall's right shoulder. Every attention was instantly procured, but he expired on Saturday evening.

98.

Duel between Mr. O'CONNELL *and Mr.*
D'ESTERRE. *February,* 1815.

THE following account is from the " Freeman's Journal," of the 2nd of February :

A difference was adjusted yesterday, at Bishop's Court, county of Kildare, which had agitated this city for several days.

At a meeting at Capel Street, on the Saturday previous to the late Aggregate Meeting, Mr. O'Connell attended, and in illustrating some matter, which he was anxious to enforce, he alluded, in a contemptuous manner to the Corporation of Dublin. " The beggarly Corporation of Dublin," was, it seems, one of the epithets of scorn used in reprobation of this act. Mr. J. N. D'Esterre is a member of the Corporation, and having seen this phrase, he addressed a letter on the 25th (the day after the Aggregate Meeting) to Mr. O'Connell, requiring to know, whether he was fairly reported. On the day after Mr. O'Connell sent an answer, in which he said, he would not avow, nor disavow, what had been reported in the newspapers. But he added, that if Mr. D'Esterre wrote to him to know his opinion of the Common Council of Dublin, as a body, he could easily satisfy him by saying, that no expression, which language could furnish, was sufficient to convey the sentiments of contempt he had for that body. Mr. O'Connell besides requested, that Mr. D'Esterre should consider his answer as forming the close of the epistolary correspondence on this topic.

On Friday, a letter was left in Merrion Square for Mr. O'Connell, during his absence at the courts. Its direction was different from the former one which came from Mr. D'Esterre; and Mr. James O'Connell, who had instructions to open any communications, that were directed to his brother in his absence, ascertained the quarter, from whence it came. He sought merely for the signature, and on perceiving it to be Mr. D'Esterre's, he immediately closed the letter, and stated in a note to Mr. D'Esterre the circumstances, under which he opened it. He said, he was ignorant of its contents, not wishing, after the request his brother had made on the day previous, to know any thing more of Mr. D'Esterre's epistolary messages. He added, that his brother did not expect to hear a second time from Mr. D'Esterre, through the medium of *a letter*. Things remained in this condition till Sunday last. On this day Mr. James O'Connell received a note from Mr. D'Esterre, containing disrespectful observations on himself and his brother. Immediately after the receipt of it, he sent his friend, Captain O'Mullan, to Mr. D'Esterre to say, that after he adjusted his affair with his brother, he would bring him to account for his conduct to himself peculiarly. Captain O'Mullan at the same time intimated, that Counsellor O'Connell was astonished at his not hearing, in what he conceived the *proper way*, from Mr. D'Esterre.

Nothing farther happened on Sunday; and on Monday morning Mr. Lidwell, who remained here several days to be the friend of Mr. O'Connell, though some members of his family were seriously indisposed, left town for home, despairing of any issue being put to the controversy. Monday passed on; and on Tuesday considerable sensation was created, by a rumour that Mr. D'Esterre was advised to go to the Four Courts, to offer Mr. O'Connell personal violence. Neither of the parties came in contact. But it seems Mr. D'Esterre was met on one of the quays by Mr. Richard O'Gorman, who remonstrated with him, by stating, that he conceived he was pursuing a very unusual sort of conduct. This occurred about three o'clock; but no challenge followed. About four it was understood that Mr. D'Esterre was on the streets; and Mr. O'Connell paraded about with one or two friends, but did not come across his antagonist. A multitude soon collected about him, among whom there could not be less than five hundred gentlemen of respectability; and Mr. O'Connell then had no resource left, than to take refuge in a house in Exchequer-street. In a short time Judge Day entered, in his magisterial capacity, to put him under arrest. The Hon. Justice said, he would be satisfied if he had the guarantee of Mr. O'Connell's honour, that he would proceed no farther in the business. "It is not my business, Mr. Justice," said Mr. O'Connell, "to be the aggressor. Further, however, I must tell you, that no human consideration will induce me to go."

The Hon. Justice then retired; and Mr. O'Connell shortly after repaired to Merrion-square. No challenge of any kind grew out of Tuesday's proceedings.

On Wednesday morning, however, it was at length intimated to Mr. O'Connell, that Mr. D'Esterre intended to call upon him for a meeting. Twelve o'clock was fixed upon for the nomination of hour and place. There was some overture made to enlarge the time, but Mr. O'Connell's friend would not consent. We should mention, that his friend was Major Macnamara, of Doolen, in the county of Clare, a protestant gentleman attached to no party, and of the highest respectability. The friend of Mr. D'Esterre was Sir Edward Stanley.

After some discussion the parties fixed upon the place, which we have already mentioned. It is about twelve miles distant from this city, and constitutes part of Lord Ponsonby's demesne. The hour appointed was half past three o'clock. At three precisely (we can speak confidently, for we now speak from personal knowledge) Mr. O'Connell, attended by his second, Surgeon Macklin, and a number of friends, was on the ground. About four, Mr. D'Esterre, attended only by Surgeon Peel, Sir Edward Stanley (his second), and a Mr. D'Esterre, of Limerick, appeared. There was some conversation between the seconds as to position, mode of fire, &c.; which, added to other sources of delay, occupied forty minutes. During this interval, Mr. D'Esterre took occasion to say, that his quarrel with Mr. O'Connell was not of a religious nature. To the Catholics, or their leaders, he said he had no animosity whatever.

At forty minutes past four, the combatants were on the ground; they both displayed the greatest coolness and courage. The friends of both parties retired, and the combatants, having a pistol in each hand, with directions to discharge them at their discretion, prepared to fire. They levelled, and before the lapse of a second, both shots were heard. Mr. D'Esterre's was first, and missed. Mr. O'Connell's followed instantaneously, and took effect in the thigh of his antagonist, about an inch above the hip. Mr. D'Esterre of course fell, and both the surgeons hastened to him. They found that the ball had " traversed the hip," and could not be found. There was an immense effusion of blood. All parties prepared to move towards home, and arrived in town before eight o'clock.

It is said, that Mr. D'Esterre's wound is very dangerous; we sincerely hope, however, that it will not prove mortal. The ball passed through both thighs. There was a violent hæmorrhage of the bladder last night, but it had ceased before morning.

We need not describe the emotions which burst forth all along the road, when it was ascertained that Mr. O'Connell was safe.

Mr. D'Esterre died at five o'clock on the third.

99.

Duel between Colonel QUENTIN *and Colonel* PALMER. *February 9, 1815.*

COLONEL PALMER had been at Bourdeaux, and on his return to Paris, on Thursday last, found that Mr. Lawrell (Colonel Quentin's brother-in-law), had left a card repeatedly at his hotel, during his absence; in consequence of which, he immediately signified his arrival to that gentleman. Mr. Lawrell soon after waited upon him, with a challenge from Colonel Quentin. The parties met; Colonel Quentin accompanied by his relative, and Colonel Palmer by Mr. T. Thompson, Member for Midhurst. The distance measured was twelve paces; and the challenger, thinking himself aggrieved, having given his first fire, Colonel Palmer shewed that he was influenced by no personal motive, by instantly discharging his pistol in the air.

Mr. Lawrell and Colonel Quentin having thereupon, in answer to an enquiry from Mr. Thompson, declared themselves perfectly satisfied, the affair terminated, and the parties returned to Paris.

The Duke de Guiche and two French surgeons were on the ground.

100.

Duel between Mr. —— and Mr. ——.
Edinburgh, Feb. 18, 1815.

ABOUT three o'clock on Monday last, a duel was fought between two gentlemen of this city, near to Caroline Park. Intimation of their intention being given to the Sheriff, a warrant was issued for their apprehension; but before the officers could reach the ground, the parties had interchanged shots without effect. They and their seconds were however taken into custody; and on enquiry into the circumstances of the case, the cause of quarrel appeared so unsatisfactory, and the whole proceeding of those concerned so very strange, that, besides ordering them to find security to keep the peace, the Sheriff fined both principals and seconds in twenty-five guineas each; and ordered the same to be applied for the benefit of the Lunatic Asylum, as being, from its nature, an institution best entitled to a fine derived from such a source.

101.

Duel between P. Dillon, *Esq. and* B. Kane, *Esq.* *Dublin, Feb.* 21, 1816.

Yesterday evening a meeting took place near Merlin Park, between P. Dillon, Esq., of this town, and B. Kane, Esq., of ——, when the former received his adversary's ball under the right breast, and instantly expired.

These two gentlemen were close friends for many years. Mr. Dillon fought several duels, in all of which Mr. Kane acted as his second. And it is remarkable that Mr. Dillon's father lost his life in an affair of honour with the late Malachy Fallon, Esq. at the same age, and nearly on the same spot where his son fell.

102.

Duel between Mr. ALLEY *and Mr.* ADOLPHUS. *December* 2, 1816.

A dispute between Mr. Alley and Mr. Adolphus, which originated in the court of the Old Bailey, during a late trial, has at length been brought to a termination, and without any fatal result.

On November 13th, Mr. Adolphus sent notice to Mr. Alley, that he would be ready to meet him at Calais as soon as ever he chose; the parties being bound over by the magistrates to preserve the peace within this kingdom. Mr. Alley accepted the challenge, and on the 14th set out for Dover, accompanied by Captain Alley, his cousin and second. Two of his intimate friends, Mr. Agar and Mr. Bevil, also, voluntarily accompanied him. They arrived at Calais on the 15th, some hours before Mr. Adolphus; and at 2 o'clock on the 16th, after the preliminary business was arranged by the seconds, the combatants met, a short distance from the town, took their ground, and on the signal being given, they both fired together. Mr. Alley was wounded in the right arm; and the ball from his pistol passed so close to his adversary, as almost to graze his head. Here the business terminated. An eminent surgeon being immediately sent for, extracted the ball from Mr. Alley's arm.

103.

Duel between Major LOCKYER *and Mr.* SUTTON COCHRANE. *Cowes, December* 12, 1817.

ON Wednesday, a duel was fought here between Major Lockyer and Mr. Sutton Cochrane, recently a lieutenant in the Royal

Navy, which proved fatal to the latter, he having received his antagonist's ball under the right breast, which passed through both ventricles of the heart and the lungs.

These gentlemen, in company with a Mr. Redesdale, and a Mr. Hand, and upwards of sixty others, were going out as adventurers to South America, in the ship Grace, Davy master, now lying in these roads, wind bound. The trifling difference between the parties arose, in consequence of an expression of an unguarded nature, from the deceased, the evening before, while regaling themselves, with several others, at an inn: he having asserted " that they were all in debt, and were seeking their fortunes." At which the Major felt very indignant, and asked, " if the other meant to include him?" The deceased replied in the affirmative, and declared, " he would prove his assertion," which he did by giving a very ingenious explanation, observing, " that if we were not in debt to any of our fellow-beings, we were all indebted to our Maker." But the Major, not considering the explanation satisfactory, insisted on Mr. Cochrane's meeting him the next morning, at the dawn of day, who very reluctantly fell into the measure, previously declaring he would not fire himself. But if his opponent insisted, he would receive his fire.

It was agreed, that they should both fire at one time, but when the signal was made, it was observed, the deceased never raised his arm to level his pistol, while the ball of his antagonist's pistol immediately struck at the seat of life. When the pistol of the deceased was examined afterwards, it was found neither unstopped nor cocked. The Major and the two seconds, Messrs. Redesdale and Hand, immediately decamped across the water.

The deceased was a well-educated and genteel young man, about twenty years of age, and we believe a relation of Lord Cochrane.

A Coroner's inquest sate upon the body, and the jury delivered their verdict, " wilful murder," against Major Lockyer, and Messrs. Redesdale and Hand, and the Coroner issued his warrant for their apprehension. Mr. Hand was apprehended (by Allen the

Newport constable,) at Portsmouth, on Thursday: the others are at large.

Major Lockyer and Mr. Hand were tried at Winchester Assizes, on the 7th of March, 1818, and the jury returning a verdict of manslaughter, they were sentenced to three months imprisonment.

104.

Duel between Mr. THEODORE O'CALLAGHAN *and Lieutenant* BAILEY. *Bow Street, January* 13, 1818.

YESTERDAY morning, between eight and nine o'clock, Mr. Theodore O'Callaghan and Lieutenant Bailey, of the 58th regiment met in a field near Chalk Farm, to fight a duel, accompanied by Mr. Charles Newbolt, and Mr. Thomas Joseph Phealan, as seconds. Lieutenant Bailey received a wound in his right side, which proved fatal, as he languished of it about two hours, and then expired. Mr. O'Callaghan and the two seconds, were afterwards taken into custody, and brought to this office, and underwent an examination before Mr. Conant, the sitting magistrate, when then the following particulars transpired.

Thomas Hunt, a constable at Hampstead, stated—That he was sent for to Mr. Adams's house, near Chalk Farm, in Ingram's Lane, near the Load of Hay, where he took the prisoners into custody, in consequence of a gentleman having been killed in a duel.

Mr. Adams, who occupies the house above alluded to, attended, and stated— That about nine o'clock that morning, he was in his bed room, in the act of dressing himself, when he heard the discharge of two pistols, which induced him to look out of his window. He saw four gentlemen two fields off his house, near Chalk Farm, whom he considered in the act of fighting a duel. As they did not separate, or disperse, he was fearful they would fire again. He, therefore, finished dressing himself with all possible speed, and hurried off to the spot, to endeavour to prevent the shot being repeated. Just as he arrived at the gate, and was in the act of getting over it, two pistols went off. He observed one of the gentlemen, who appeared to have discharged one of the pistols, to turn round, and concluded he had received one of the shots. The other three gentlemen, the prisoners, went up to him instantly, two of them supported him on each side, to prevent him from falling. Each of them held an arm. On the witness getting up to them, one of them said to him, " they were all friends." He saw blood running down the trowsers of the deceased profusely. The three prisoners gave him their names and addresses. He did not see a pistol in the possession of the deceased, or any of the prisoners. He invited the prisoners to conduct the deceased to his house, which they accordingly did. He did not observe any other person in the field, where the parties were, or near the spot. He observed to the parties, that it was an unfortunate affair. They all agreed, it was so. They enquired of him, if there was a house near for the prisoners to conduct the deceased to, as they were fearful of putting him to inconvenience. However, there being no public house near, they supported him to his house, which was about four or five hundred yards off.

The deceased appeared to him to be in a dangerous state, and blood was running out of his trowsers very fast. A surgeon was sent for, with all possible speed. The deceased was laid on a sofa in his parlour, and while he was lying there, he desired Mr. Theodore O'Callaghan to come to him, and held out his hand to shake hands with him, and said, "he had behaved most honourably." The deceased had observed, that he was sensible he was dying, and could not live long. After this, he called the other two prisoners to him, shook hands with them, and made similar observations to them, and said, " he forgave them all."

Mr. O'Callaghan, after this, went off to Hampstead, to get a coach to convey him from his house. But in the mean time, Mr. Rodd, a surgeon of Hampstead, arrived in about half an hour from the time of the fatal shot. Mr. Rodd, after having examined the wound, said it was impossible to remove him. The shot had entered on his right side, passed through his intestines, and all but came through on the left side, it being only confined by the skin. It was visible to the eye. The shot had carried with it a piece of the cloth of his coat, and other garments.

The deceased had observed to him, that the quarrel which had been the cause of the duel, was not originally a quarrel of their own, but had sprung out of a quarrel of their mutual friends, who were to have fought a duel yesterday, and they were to have been their seconds. Upon recollection, he would not be positive whether it was the deceased or Mr. O'Callaghan, who made this observation. He, however, understood that it was the prisoner O'Callaghan, who shot the deceased. He did not observe any pistols in the possession of either of the parties, but he found two pistols lying on the table of his parlour; none of them owned them; but he had no doubt of their belonging to them (they were produced in the office in an unloaded state) they were of a large size. There were no pistols there before they came into the house. The deceased lived about two hours, or two hours and a quarter. All the prisoners paid every possible attention to the deceased, during the time he lived. He conversed with them all, and particularly with Mr. P. Phealan, who, the deceased told the witness, had been his second, or his friend, he could not recollect which. He heard him request Mr. Phealan to write to his father the full particulars of the whole affair, and who, he understood, lived at Limerick.

Mr. Phealan had some conversation with the deceased privately, every other person having left the room. He then went off to London to procure more surgical assistance. On his return, the deceased had expired. Mr. Newbolt went, in the mean time, to enquire for lodgings at Chalk Farm, or the neighbourhood. Mr. O'Callaghan went to Hampstead to procure a coach. They all appeared anxious to do every thing for the deceased, and did not seem inclined to abscond, but very readily surrendered themselves.

The prisoners were not called upon for any defence. The magistrate informed them, the law did not make any distinction in cases of murder, all being considered as principals. They must all, therefore, be detained. It was suggested to the magistrate, that safe custody was all, probably, that he would require, to which he assented, and it was agreed, that they should be kept in the watch-house, till the decision of the Coroner's inquest is known; when it was suggested by the magistrate, that it was probable he would admit Mr. Phealan to bail. He regretted that the surgeon had not attended.

Public Office, Bow Street.

Yesterday morning, another investigation took place before Richard Birnie, Esq. respecting the cause of the death of Lieutenant Edward Bailey, of the 58th regiment. Mr. George Rodd, the surgeon of Hampstead, who had omitted to attend the examination on Monday evening, attended yesterday morning, and stated, That he was sent for on Monday morning, with great speed, to go to Mr. Adams's house in Ingram's Lane, to attend a gentleman, who had been severely wounded. He arrived at Mr. Adams's house about ten o'clock, where he saw a gentleman, who had been wounded, lying on a sofa. He proceeded to examine the wound, and he found a ball had penetrated on his right side, very nearly in a line with his navel. He proceeded to examine him on his left side, when he discovered that a ball was resting between his skin and the muscles. He succeeded in extracting the ball from the wound, and then dressed it. The three gentlemen, who are the prisoners, were present in the room at the time he examined the wounds of the deceased. After Lieutenant Bailey died, he opened the body, and found his intestines had been wounded in three different places, and which he had no doubt had caused his death.

Mr. William Adams, who has acted so humanely in this unfortunate transaction, attended again, and stated, in addition to the testimony which he gave on Monday evening,—That after the deceased had called Mr. O'Callaghan to him on the sofa, and shook hands with him, and said every thing had been conducted in the most honourable manner, and that he forgave him—he asked Mr. O'Callaghan if he would have done the same by him if he had wounded him? To this Mr. O'Callaghagan replied, Most certainly, he should have acted as he had done; and followed up the observation by saying, "I wish I had been wounded instead of you."

Mr. O'Callaghan appeared much affected, and said, " You touched me in the first fire we had on one of my legs, by what is called a graze." He then exhibited his trowsers and boots; when it appeared, that a ball had passed through both the legs of his trowsers, and one of his boots. He saw the deceased, Lieutenant Bailey, shake hands very heartily with Mr. O'Callaghan, previous to their parting.

The three prisoners were ordered to be detained in custody.

On the application of an attorney engaged for the prisoners, Mr. Birnie agreed to their undergoing another investigation previous to their commitment for trial; and the attorney wrote to Mr. Adams, requesting it as a favour that he would attend again last evening at seven o'clock, at which hour the three prisoners were brought again to this office; and Mr. Birnie having taken his seat on the bench, Mr. Nolan, Mr. Arabin, and another barrister, whose name we understood to be Gould, presented themselves to the magistrate in behalf of the prisoners.

Mr. Nolan first addressed the magistrate,

and observed, that as the Coroner's inquest had not yet sate, and would not sit till to-morrow, as the prisoners were now in safe custody, the magistrate would let them remain where they had hitherto been confined; as he well knew it was in vain to urge any discretionary power of the magistrate, as to bailing them, till the decision of the Coroner's jury was known.

The learned gentleman said, he felt strongly the charge of the crime under which the prisoners laboured; but he would say, that nothing he had heard of the evidence against them, in the least affected them as to premeditated murder. With regard to one of the prisoners, Mr. Phealan, he was the particular friend of the deceased, and was by no means instrumental to the violence that had been committed. All that Mr. Adams said respecting him, and who was the most material witness, was, that he was there on the spot at the time that the deceased came by his death. For any thing that appeared in evidence, he might have been there accidentally; the spot where the transaction took place being near a public road and a path, he might have been an idle spectator. He must now answer for the highest crime which the law knew. The question he had to urge was, whether he was to remain in custody, or be admitted to bail, till his trial; which he urged as to a sense of honour and humanity, and which he had no doubt was possessed by the gentleman by whom the business was first investigated, Mr. Conant; and if he had then been present, he should have taken the liberty of asking Mr. Adams a few questions, which he flattered himself would have induced the magistrate to have admitted the gentlemen to bail. If the Coroner's inquest had met and pronounced their verdict, the case would be altered. As Mr. Adams had not arrived, he trusted there would be no objection to let them remain where they were. To meet his fate, it was the wish of his friend, Mr. O'Callaghan, as soon as possible, and to whom the trial would be the most interesting; and he by no means wished to defer it. All he wished for was, that they might be remanded till tomorrow morning. After the Coroner's inquest had sate upon the body of Lieutenant Bailey, and returned a verdict, it would then be a question, whether all or any of the gentlemen should be admitted to bail.

Mr. Arabin followed Mr. Nolan, and very handsomely acknowledged the kindness which had been shewn him, in allowing him to read the evidence which had been taken in writing against his clients. He proceeded to enlarge upon it, and urged that there was not a shadow of difference between Mr. Phealan and Mr. Newbolt; and solicited that their commitment may be deferred, and that they may be admitted to bail.

Mr. Birnie in reply, said, it was his wish to do justice to all; the prisoners had all been found on the spot.

Mr. Arabin admitted, that there was no doubt about that; but he appealed to the magistrate to feel as a man, a gentleman, and as a lawyer.

Mr. Birnie said, he had a public duty to perform. In answer to the arguments of the learned counsel, he quoted the celebrated case of Montgomery and Macnamara, in which Mr. Heaviside, the surgeon, was committed to Newgate, who had only been attending professionally; yet he was committed on a charge of murder. In that case, it will be recollected, Sir Richard Ford was committing magistrate, who at that time took up the practice of duelling in a very spirited manner; and publicly expressed his determination to commit the surgeon, and all persons who were present at fatal duels, to take their trials for murder. And it was this firm conduct in the magistrate at that time, which checked the spirit of duelling for some time after; Mr. Heaviside being confined in Newgate for a considerable time, and at a very heavy expense. Probably bail to any amount could have been procured for Mr. Heaviside, but all was refused.

The other learned counsel was heard in favour of the prisoners.

Mr. Nolan said, their only motive for the application in behalf of the prisoners was, that they would be more comfortable where they had been, during the night, than in Newgate.

Mr. Birnie observed, that he did not know that magistrates had any thing to do with Coroners inquests.

Mr. Nolan said, that if the magistrate

complied with the application, no mischief, public or private, could happen.

The magistrate observed, that it was in evidence before him that one of the King's subjects had been deprived of life; and upon prima facie evidence it was murder.

Mr. Nolan again urged his motive, that his clients might have a more comfortable lodging.

Mr. Birnie said, he had now made up his mind; the prisoners must all be committed to Newgate, to take their trials for the murder of Lieutenant Bailey; and he was convinced that the three learned gentlemen would allow that he had decided right.

The gentlemen bowed and retired.

The prisoners were given into the custody of the officers, to be conveyed to Newgate.

January 14, 1818.

AT the ensuing sessions at the Old Bailey, these three gentlemen were tried for the crime laid to their charge; when the jury having returned a verdict of "manslaughter," they were sentenced to be imprisoned three months in Newgate.

105.

Duel between Lieutenant CARTWRIGHT *and Lieutenant* MAXWELL. *March*, 1818.

ON the first instant, a fatal duel took place at Avaranches, on the opposite coast. It arose in consequence of a dispute between Lieutenants Cartwright and Maxwell, of the royal navy. They met on Saturday morning, at a little distance from Avaranches. Mr. Cartwright received his adversary's first fire; the ball entered his forehead, and he expired in a few moments.

A few weeks since he was married in St. Hilier's, to Miss Man, niece to the late Bishop of Cork and Ross.

106.

Duel between Captain N. *and Lieutenant* L. *April* 2, 1818.

A dispute arose respecting a lady, at Covent Garden theatre, on Monday night, between Captain N., of the royal navy, and Lieutenant L., of a foot regiment.

A meeting was appointed at Chalk Farm,

at six o'clock on Tuesday morning. The parties, with their seconds, attended; the ground was measured, eight paces being the distance fixed. The parties fired together by signal, but both shots proved harmless: they fired again, when Lieutenant L.'s ball grazed Captain N.'s head, but fortunately did not seriously injure him. By the interposition of the seconds, an amicable adjustment of the affair took place, and the parties left the ground friends.

107.

Duel between Captain F—r—b *and* G. R. R——k, *Esq. April,* 1818.

A duel took place last week between Captain F—r—b and G. R. R——k, Esq., in consequence of a dispute at one of the Surrey hunting balls. The latter gentleman was wounded slightly in the body in the second fire. The Captain is on the point of marrying with his sister; and they parted good friends.

108.

Duel between Lieutenant GORDON *and a French Officer. Cambray, April* 14, 1818.

LIEUTENANTS Gordon and M., of the Guards, on the evening of the 31st of March, were walking on the Esplanade; some other officers joined them, stopping to enter into conversation. At this moment a Frenchman, having the appearance of an officer, passed them several times very closely, making very short turns, and though no sort of provocation had been offered, staring them full in the face in the most insolent manner; yet no notice whatever was taken of his conduct.

The officers then separated; Lieutenants Gordon and M. walked away arm in arm. As they passed the Frenchman, he made use of the grossest epithets; when Lieutenant Gordon, in the mildest manner, enquired if such expressions were intended for them? The French officer's reply was, " Prenez cela comme vous voulez; si vous le prenez pour vous, tenez le donc." " You may receive them as you please; if you suppose them meant for you, take them,"

Cards were then exchanged, and a meeting took place the following morning. The French Officer, when called upon by Lieutenant M. to retract his words, refused to do so; though he had acknowledged to the commissaire de police on the previous evening, that he had misconducted himself, promising to make an apology. The parties having taken their ground, at the first fire the Frenchman's shot took effect, the ball passing through Mr. Gordon's body, and he instantaneously expired.

Since the unfortunate affair, it has been discovered that this French officer is a systematic duellist; and it is known that he publicly declared in a coffee-house, that he would take the life of some English officer. He is in active service, belonging to the Legion du Nord, and came to Cambray to see his friends. To three different parties he gave a different name. It was the unfortunate lot of Lieutenant Gordon to fall a victim to the national prejudice of a ruffian; and at the early age of twenty, has his country been deprived of a young officer, who, from his rising talents and characteristic bravery, promised to be one of its fairest ornaments, both as a gentleman, and a soldier.

109.

Duel between Lieutenant PICKFORD *and* M. MARINIER. *Caen, April* 26, 1818.

A fatal duel took place this day, between Lieutenant Pickford and M. Marinier, in consequence of a dispute, arising out of quarrels between other parties, English and French, at Caen.

Lieutenant Morgan, of the navy, was second to Lieutenant Pickford; and M. Dubuisson, one of the original disputants, to M. Marinier. There was some dispute about distances: Marinier wanted fifteen paces; Pickford said he was no shot, and would allow of none beyond four. To this Marinier had no objection, provided he had the first fire. Pickford insisted they should fire together; but this was stiffly opposed. Another proposal was then made, that Marinier's friend should charge one only of his pistols with ball, and give Pickford the choice; or, that Morgan should charge with ball one of his pair, and should let Marinier choose. This was acceded to: Marinier first took one, and then Pickford the other. They presented together; the interval between them was about two feet. After a moment or two of hesitation the word was given, and Pickford's ball struck under his adversary's ribs on the right side, and passed through his body; he presently expired.

110.
Duel between Mr. M. and Mr. B—n. May 7, 1818.

In consequence of a dispute at a gaming house on Monday night, in the vicinity of Piccadilly, Mr. M., who was an officer in the British service, at Brussels, and Mr. B—n, a medical man, met at three in the morning on Tuesday, in the King's Road. They fought at twelve paces. Mr. B. was wounded on the back of the hand, and the affair was adjusted.

111.

Duel between Captain DOBBYN *and Mr.* FELLOWES. *May*, 1818.

IN consequence of an insult offered to Captain Dobbyn (late of the 5th Dragoon Guards), on Friday last, in the Court of King's Bench, the parties met yesterday morning in Epping Forest, attended by Mr. C. A. Cooke for Mr. Fellowes, and by Colonel Macirone for Captain Dobbyn. Shots were exchanged without effect, when further proceedings were prevented, by Mr. Cooke declaring his determination to quit the ground, conceiving that what had passed was sufficient to frame a satisfactory explanation upon. This explanation could not be adjusted; on which Captain Dobbyn and his friend insisted on repeating the fire, to which Mr. Fellowes most readily agreed; but his second, Mr. Cooke, adhering to his original determination of quitting the field, rendered any farther proceedings of Captain Dobbyn and his second impossible.

112.

Duel beween Lieutenant WILLIAMS, *R. N.* *and Mr.* WALCOT. *June* 21, 1818.

A meeting took place on Tuesday morning, at eleven o'clock, at Chalk Farm, between Lieutenant Williams of the Royal Navy, and Mr. Walcot. The parties exchanged shots twice, and on the last fire, Mr. Walcot received a wound in his left arm. The seconds then interfered, and the parties left the ground on friendly terms.

The meeting originated in a dispute at Vauxhall Gardens, on the Wednesday sen'-night.

113.

Duel between his Excellency the Count of C——HA *and Major* MACKINTOSH, *both Officers of Cavalry. July* 5, 1818.

DUEL and attempt to assassination. A duel lately took place in Lisbon, between his Excellency the Count of C——ha and an English officer of that service, Major R. Mackintosh; both officers of cavalry, in consequence of an insult offered by the former to a Portuguese lady of nobility, whilst under the arm of the latter at San Carlos. It appears they met with the sabre, and that the British officer completely beat the Count to the ground, and that he could not be compelled to rally and combat. The affray ended in a disgraceful manner on the part of the Count, who with six ruffians employed for the purpose, afterwards made an attempt to assassinate the gallant Major and his second, on their return from a party, but who entirely failed in the attempt. This conduct has produced a considerable sensation in Lisbon, and called forth the just indignation of all, particularly the females of his own nation.

114.

Duel in America, between Dr. BACON *and Dr.* JOHN S. HARDAWAY.

FATAL occurrence.—We understand, says the Petersbourgh Republican of July the 7th, that at Nottaway Court-house, on Tuesday, it being a court day, a rencontre took place between Dr. Bacon, son of Major Bacon, and Dr. John S. Hardaway, in which each party used the dirk. Dr. Hardaway was mortally wounded, and expired on Sunday. Dr. Bacon was wounded in three places, but his wounds are not considered fatal. We are not informed of the particulars of this rencontre.

115.

Duel between Mr. WALLACE *and Mr.* VANHOMRIGHT. *July* 19, 1818.

ON Sunday week Mr. Wallace and Mr. Vanhomright met in the neighbourhood of the Man of War, near Dublin, in consequence of a transaction of the preceding day, when, after discharging each a case of pistols, they quitted the ground, attended by their seconds. Mr. Grattan, Jun. accompanied Mr. Wallace, and Major Cheshire, Mr. Vanhomright. Neither parties received the slightest injury.

116.

Duel between Mr. SEARLE *and Mr.* PURVER. *July* 19, 1818.

ON Tuesday week, a meeting took place near South-sea Castle, between Mr. Searle, son of Captain Searle, C. B. Royal Navy, and Mr. Purver, midshipman of his Majesty's sloop Leveret. At the first fire the former gentleman received a severe wound in the left hand, in consequence of which the parties left the ground. Mr. Searle's pistol missed fire.

The ball was extracted immediately by the surgeon's mate of the above sloop.

117.

Duel between Mr. LUKE WHITE *and Captain* CONALLY. *July* 26, 1818.

AT the Leitrim Election, a duel was fought between young Mr. Luke White and Captain Conally of the Leitrim Militia. The latter received a ball in the shoulder.

118.

Duel between Lieut. RADWELL, *R. N. and Mr.* FRAME. *August* 9, 1818.

A meeting took place on Tuesday morning, about 7 o'clock, at Chalk Farm, between Mr. Radwell of the Royal Navy, and Mr. Frame; when the parties fired by signal, at a distance of eight paces.

Mr. Frame received his antagonist's ball in his left arm; he was immediately conveyed home, when surgical aid was given, and he is now sufficiently recovered to leave his room.

119.

Duel between Mr. HILLSON *and Mr.* MARSDEN. *September* 13, 1818.

A duel was fought on Hounslow Heath, on Monday morning, between two gentlemen named Hillson and Marsden, which arose out of a dispute in one of the stands at Egham races. The latter was wounded severely on the left side, and was conveyed away in a gig. Some peace-officers had followed the parties from Old Oak Common, where they first met, but were too late to prevent the mischief.

120.

Duel between Mr. B—— and Mr. W——.
September 13, 1818.

A few days since a duel was fought between Gravelines and Calais, by two English gentleman; a Mr. B—— and a Mr. W——. They fired one shot each, when Mr. B. received the ball of his antagonist in the pistol hand, which took off two of his fingers; the seconds then interfered, and the dispute was settled. The difference occurred in England, from whence the parties arrived, and on the affair being terminated, they quitted France for that country.

121.

Duel prevented. September 27, 1818.

INFORMATION having been received that a duel was to have taken place yesterday, on Wormwood Scrubs, between two gentlemen on the staff, Mr. M—n—g and Mr. G—g—n, they had scarcely arrived at the spot, when the constables appeared and prevented the same. No breach of the peace having taken place, they were suffered to depart.

122.

Duel between Sir J. G. EGERTON *and* LORD BELGRAVE. *November* 1, 1818.

AN affair of honour was decided on Saturday fortnight, on the Flats near Chester, between Sir J. G. Egerton and Lord Belgrave. On the first fire Sir John's ball struck Lord Belgrave in the pistol arm, but his lordship was not dangerously wounded, and is doing well. The cause of quarrel between the parties originated, we understand, in certain proceedings which took place the day preceding, at the annual election of mayor for the city of Chester. A Mr. Baker, in proposing Mr. Evans, who is in the Government interest, as mayor, made what were considered rather pointed allusions to some of the Egerton party, and insinuated that they had been stimulated by Sir J. Egerton himself.

The insinuation was required by Sir John to be disavowed by Lord Belgrave, who was present, but this his lordship refused. The greatest confusion then arose in the assembly, and the Recorder was ultimately obliged to adjourn the court to another day. The meeting between Sir J. and Lord Belgrave was immediately afterwards arranged.

123.

Duel between the EARL OF H—— *and* LORD W——. *November* 29, 1818.

A meeting took place at Chalk Farm, on Wednesday morning, between two young noblemen, the Earl of H—— and Lord W——, attended by two noble friends, the Earl of B—— and Lord F——; after an exchange of shots, the seconds interfered, and a reconciliation took place.

124.

Duel between Mr. H—E—Y *and Captain* E—N—N. *January* 10, 1819.

A duel was fought on Thursday morning, on Finchley Common, between Mr. H—e—y a surgeon, and Captain E—n—n, which arose in consequence of a dispute about Mrs. C——e, a celebrated beauty, dashing in life. The Captain was slightly wounded, and the affair ended.

125.

Duel between F. A. R——N, *Esq. and* Mr. F—MER. *February* 21, 1819.

A duel took place on Tuesday morning, on Wimbledon Common, between F. A. R——n, Esq. of the Kent-road, and Mr. F—mer, belonging to the staff, when the latter was wounded, it was feared, dangerously, by the ball entering his right side. The dispute originated at the Opera on Saturday night.

126.

Duel between General MASON *and Mr.* M'CARTY, *in America*. *April* 4, 1819.

INCORRECT reports being current respecting the interviews and communications between the respective friends of General

Mason and Mr. M'Carthy, it is thought proper to state:

1st. That on presenting the challenge two modes of terminating the affair were proposed by Mr. M'Carthy; first, to fight on a barrel of powder; and secondly, to fight with dirks: both which were objected to, as not according with the established usages, as being without exemple, and as calculated to establish a dangerous precedent.

2nd. That a third mode was proposed in the following written acceptance of the challenge; to which the seconds of General Mason were bound to accede, both from the positive instructions of their principal, and from the laws which govern the settlement of disputes in the field of honour.

"Gentlemen,——I agree to meet and fight your friend, General A. T. Mason, to-morrow evening, five o'clock, at Montgomery Court-House. As I am at liberty to select the weapon with which I am to fight, I beg leave to propose a musket charged with buck shot, and at the distance of ten feet. J. M. M'CARTHY.

"*February* 4, 1819."

3rd. That it was proposed by the friends of General Mason, and agreed to by the friends of Mr. M'Carthy, to substitute a single ball for buck shot.

4th. That it was agreed by the friends of both parties to postpone the meeting until 10 o'clock on Saturday morning; and that, on the ground, the distance measured exceeded twelve feet.

It now only remains to state, that all reports respecting the indecorous deportment of either party on the ground, are entirely false; that the unfortunate meeting took place at the appointed time, and that the affair, although fatally, was honourably terminated.

It has been reported that General Mason was struck with three balls. At the request of his friends, the executors of General Mason consented to an examination of the body; and after a minute dissection, it was clearly ascertained that but one ball had entered the deceased.

127.

Duel between Captain JOHNSTON, 64*th Regiment, and* BENJAMIN T. BROWNE, *Surgeon of the Erie, American Sloop of War.* June 6, 1819.

ON the 23d of March, while Captain Johnston was on the main-guard duty at Gibraltar, a report was made to him that five individuals had been taken into custody by a sentry, on their way home from the play, for being without lights, contrary to the garrison regulations. Captain Johnston immediately ordered a sufficient number of men to see them home. In about ten minutes afterwards the police serjeant, who accompanied them, returned with three of them in custody; and acquainted Captain Johnston that Archibald Taylor had endeavoured to escape from the sentry, and had made use of the most provoking and abusive language to him. Having, upon enquiry, found the report to be correct, Captain Johnston ordered the offender to be confined in the Crib; an order which he resisted most violently, and used very offensive language to Captain Johnston himself. At this time Captain Johnston was not at all apprised this was an American. Taylor demanded satisfaction for the treatment he had received; but Captain Johnston considered that he had merely acted in conformity with his duty, and paying no attention to Mr. Taylor, reported the whole affair to the Field Officer, who approved of the course that had been pursued, and ordered Taylor to be continued in confinement. In the morning Mr. Taylor was released; and upon the circulation of a report, two days afterwards, that Captain Johnston had declined to meet Mr. Taylor, or the American Consul, who was said to have offered "to stand in his shoes," the former having been obliged to sail immediately with the vessel, of which he was master, Captain J. applied to the Consul for an explanation; when that gentleman, in the most handsome manner, disavowed any knowledge of the reports in question, and offered Captain J. his thanks for the delicate and gentlemanly conduct which he had evinced in the business.

Thus matters continued till the evening

of the 31st of March, when Captain J. received the following letter from the hands of Lieutenant Stockton, first Lieutenant of the American sloop of war, Erie.

"*Erie Sloop, March* 31, 1819.

"Sir,

"You have refused to give the satisfaction due to a man of honour, when you did not hesitate to insult, because he was not more than a commander of an American merchant schooner. That gentleman is known to me, and I vouch for his equality to you in any respect you may choose. I am his representative, and the satisfaction I understand you boast to have offered his friends, I demand as an American; my rank, I trust, is enough for any man of honour; and you will do me the favour to consider the bearer, my friend, for your use.

(*Signed*) Benjamin T. Browne."

Mr. Browne, it appeared, was surgeon of the Erie. Captain Johnston instantly accepted the challenge; and the next morning, at eight o'clock, a meeting took place between him and Mr. Browne, upon the neutral ground (Captain J. had distinctly disavowed having made any boast whatever with regard to Mr. Taylor). The arrangement made by their mutual friends on the ground was — distance eight paces the word to be given, " Are you ready, gentlemen ?" and, on assent being given, both to fire, after a pause for taking aim while one, two, three, could be counted, or about half second time. On the first fire Captain J. received his opponent's ball through his hat. They were handed pistols a second time, and the word was given as in the previous discharge. Captain Johnston fired; but Mr. Browne reserved his fire so long, that the friend of the former exclaimed, " That is not fair," on which he fired. Captain Johnston expressed his indignation at the reservation of fire by his antagonist; and after some warm language on both sides, the third discharge took place, without effect; and on the fourth, (which was rather hurried, in consequence of the approach of a serjeant's guard,) Captain J.'s ball took effect in Mr. Browne's thigh. His friend, Mr. Stockton, immediately took up the ground, desiring Captain J. to keep his. They were about proceeding, when the serjeant's guard reached the spot, and prevented any further progress at that time.

Mr. Stockton insisted on meeting Captain Johnston the next morning, at five o'clock; to which the latter agreed, and returned to the garrison. Captain J. was prevented from meeting in the morning, from the circumstance of his having been put under arrest, and an order of garrison being made, that no officer should be permitted to pass the barriers, in coloured clothes or otherwise: he however contrived to elude the vigilance of the guard in the afternoon; and at half past four met Mr. Stockton at St. Michael's Cave.

The seconds instantly entered into conversation as to the mode of firing. Mr. Stockton's friend proposed that they should, on receiving the word, as at the first meeting, take an unlimited time for aim; this was objected to by Captain J.'s friend as sanguinary, and at variance with those principles of honour, upon which the desire of such meetings was founded.

Some argument followed, which ended in a determination to decide by chance which mode should be adopted; the result was favourable to the more humane course; but the time which was lost in this dispute, exposed them to the interruption of the guard, which was now seen approaching. It was now discovered that Mr. Stockton had no pistols, and one of Captain Johnston's was borrowed for his use. Having taken their ground at the former distance of eight paces, Mr. Stockton proceeded to take a steady aim, by resting the barrel of his pistol on his left hand. Captain Johnston's friend objected to this; and again the American endeavoured by argument to justify that very unusual mode of deciding such matters. At length the guard was seen within a hundred paces, and Captain Johnston desired that the affair might proceed in the usual manner: this was agreed to, and the discharge took place; the ball of Lieutenant Stockton's pistol passed through Captain Johnston's great coat; and before a second fire could take place, the guard came up and interfered.

The Americans then went away; and Mr. Stockton's friend declared to the officer who had accompanied him to the Ragged Staff, his perfect satisfaction at the whole proceedings. This appears to be the whole that passed with regard to Captain Johnston's affair; and certainly have no hesitation in saying, that throughout, his conduct was most honourable to himself, both as an officer and a gentleman.

128.

Duel between Captain FREETH, 64*th Regiment, and Mr.* MONTGOMERY, *of the American Sloop of War, Erie. June* 6, 1819.

THE second source of quarrel with Ensign Nutt is thus described: Whilst Ensign Nutt was lying on the guard bed, about nine o'clock on the evening of the 29th of March, a man came in and asked if the United States boat was at the landing place. Mr. Nutt said she had been there about an hour before, but concluded she was gone off. The man then asked if he might be permitted to hail her; and if she was there, if the Ensign would lower the draw-bridge. To both of these questions Mr. Nutt answered in the affirmative. The man then went out and shut the door, his appearance and demeanour were altogether unlike those of an officer, or a gentleman.

After hailing two or three times, he returned to the guard-room, and said, that as the boat was not there, he concluded he might walk up and down until she arrived; Mr. Nutt answered, "Yes, certainly," upon which the man, without any further conversation, said, "You have not treated me like a gentleman; you have remained laying down, without attempting to get up to receive me." He then added that his name was Humfries; that he was purser of the United States frigate, and as good a gentleman as Mr. Nutt: that he had never been treated so before; that he would have personal satisfaction in the morning, and concluded by demanding Mr. Nutt's card. Mr. Nutt, who was utterly ignorant that the man standing before him, was an officer, immediately said that his name was unimportant, he was an officer of the 64th, and commanded that guard for the night. He added, that being there on duty, it was not his business, or his intention, to enter into personal quarrels with individuals, and that if such language was repeated, he should send the intruder to the main-guard. Mr. Humfries then went out; when another American came in to light his segar, which he was permitted to do; and went out. Ensign Nutt then asked if the purser of the United States frigate was gone; upon which Mr. Humfries re-entered, accompanied by the person who had lighted the segar. Mr. Nutt then said, that he was willing to attribute his former irritation to his being somewhat intoxicated (which appeared to be the fact), and had no desire to send him to the main-guard, if that were the case. The other replied in the same threatening language, and again went out. A report of these occurrences was made to the field-officer of the day. At half-past ten in the morning a person waited on Mr. Nutt, who appeared to be the same that had lighted his segar the preceding night: he said his name was Montgomery, that he was surgeon of the sloop Erie; and that he had come to demand satisfaction for the insult offered to Mr. Humfries the preceding night. He concluded by desiring a meeting at the Crown and Anchor Tavern in one hour.

Mr. Nutt said he should certainly be at the place appointed; but added, that as he had reported the circumstance officially to the Governor, through the field officer of the day, he did not feel himself justified in making a personal affair of it. Captain Freeth came into the room immediately afterwards, to whom, as well as to Lieutenant Walsh, he communicated what had passed; they were of opinion that Mr. Nutt should report the matter to Major Bishop, and by no means to meet Mr. Humfries, as the whole transaction was of a public nature, and occurred whilst on duty, Mr. Nutt followed his advice, and was put under arrest by Colonel M'Donald, in consequence of which he wrote the following letter to Mr. Montgomery:

" Sir,

" In reply to your communication of this morning, I have to inform you, that having already reported the occurrence of last evening to the governor, through the field officer of the day, I am precluded from making a personal affair of what took place when in the execution of my duty. I have further to add, that I have pursued a similar course with your message delivered to me this morning. I have been guided in this measure by the advice of such of my brother officers, as I have consulted on the occasion.

"I am Sir, &c.

"A. NUTT."

Captain Freeth was the bearer of this note to Mr. Montgomery, who made use of very gross language upon the refusal of Mr. Nutt to meet Mr. Humfries, and desired Captain F. to say, that as Mr. Humfries was going to sail immediately, he would stand in his shoes. In the afternoon Mr. Montgomery and a Lieutenant of the Erie called at Mr. Nutt's quarters, and after some conversation with Captain Freeth and Lieutenant Walsh, went away with an understanding, that as soon as Ensign Nutt was out of arrest he would meet him. In the conversation with Captain Freeth, Mr. Montgomery had applied the epithet "coward," to Mr. Nutt; which, as his friend, Captain Freeth determined to resent, and accordingly met Mr. Montgomery next morning, and was wounded. This was the first which Mr. Nutt had heard of the aspertion cast upon his character, and being determined to run the risk of the loss of his commission, rather than to submit to it, he sent to demand satisfaction to the author of the calumny; and appointed a meeting on the rock. Mr. Montgomery's friend landed according to this invitation, and told Captain Dickson, Mr. Nutt's friend, Mr. Montgomery would not meet Mr. Nutt, as he considered himself absolved from his engagement with Mr. N. in consequence of his having met his friend, Captain Freeth. The next day the Erie sailed, and thus terminated the whole affair. From this it will be seen, that Mr. Nutt was as little to blame as Captain Johnston, and that in point of gallantry, where the honour of a friend was attacked, the British officers were quite as forward to become their champion as the citizens of America. While we lament that these disputes should have arisen, we cannot help observing, that the conduct of the officers of the 64th, was such as to entitle them to the approbation of their fellow soldiers throughout the empire.

129.

Duel between C. J. ALLINGHAM, *Esq. and* J. O'NEILL, *Esq.* *June* 27, 1819.

A meeting took place near Ballyshannon, county of Leitrim, on the morning of Friday, the 11th instant, between C. J. Allingham, Esq. and J. O'Neill, Esq. the former attended by Captain Coleman, and the latter by Terrence Connolly, Esq. After an exchange of two shots each, without injury to either party, a reconciliation took place.

130.

Duel between Lieut. L—L—A—s *and* P. R. M—I—G, *Esq.* *July* 18, 1819.

An affair of honour took place on Tuesday morning in Kilburn fields, between Lieutenant L—l—a—s and Mr. P. R. M—i—g, the cause of which originated in a dispute at play on Monday evening. The first shot missed: and in the second fire the Lieutenant was wounded in the thick part of the left arm. Information was received of this meeting too late to prevent it.

131.

Duel between Captain KIRSOFF *and* W. PAYTON, *Esq.* *July* 18, 1819.

Carrick on Shannon, July 4.

ON Saturday evening a meeting took place at Kittaughart, within two miles of this town, between Captain Kirsoff, late of the 20th foot, and W. Payton, Esq. Jun. of Arma in this county. Mr. Payton's ball entered Captain Kirsoff's right hip, and lodged in his left groin; it was shortly afterwards extracted by Surgeon Brady, but we are sorry to say, with little hope of recovery.

132.

Duel between Mr. UNIACKE *and Mr.* BOWIE. *August* 22, 1819.

A duel was fought at Halifax (N. S.) on the 1st instant, between Mr. Uniacke (son of the Attorney General) and Mr. Bowie, an auctioneer, when the latter was killed on the spot. The deceased had been under a prosecution for an offence, in which cause he considered Mr. Uniacke, as the prosecuting attorney, had used improper expressions regarding him, and therefore called him out to the above ordeal.

133.

Duel between Lieutenant P—— *and Captain* D——. *September* 12, 1819.

Cork, August 31.

A duel took place yesterday morning, near the Slough, between Lieutenant P—— and Captain D——; in which the former gentleman was shot through the body. He was taken to the South Infirmary, where he now lies in a dangerous state.

134.

Duel between Captain Hussey *and Lieut.* Osborn, *both of the* 38*th Regiment. September* 26, 1819.

A duel took place the 24th May last, between Captain Hussey and Lieutenant Osborn, both of the 38th regiment, on Table Mountain, Cape of Good Hope, when Captain Hussey received his adversary's ball in the left shoulder, which came out between the fourth and fifth ribs, and instantly expired.

The seconds then placed him erect against a tree, and dropping an anonymous note, in one of the officers rooms, the body was found as described in it.

135.

Duel between CHARLES PHILLIPS, *Esq. and* —— HENRIQUES, *Esq.* *Oct.* 10, 1819.

On Monday afternoon at four o'clock, a meeting took place within a mile of Cheltenham, on the Winchcomb road, between Charles Phillips, Esq. of the Irish Bar, attended by Colonel O'Neill, and —— Henriques, Esq. attended by Major Penrice, when, after an exchange of shots, the affair terminated; and before leaving the ground, the parties shook hands.

136.

Duel between two Naval Officers, HAWKINS *and* FRAZER. *October* 10, 1819.

Two English naval officers named Hawkins and Frazer, fought a duel near Boulogne, in which the former received a ball in the abdomen; the seconds were Englishmen.

137.

Duel between Captain PELLEW, 1*st Life Guards, and Lieut.* WALSH. *October* 17, 1819.

Paris, October 12.

You will, ere this, have heard the fatal termination of Captain Pellew's guilty attachment to the wife of Mr. Walsh.

Mr. W. not long since exchanged from the Life Guards, in which corps Captain P. held his commission. Previous to Mr. W.'s quitting the regiment, he had resided with his wife a good deal in the barracks in Hyde Park, when, being young and thoughtless, she unhappily received with too much readiness those attentions which military men often thinks themselves at liberty to pay to every female. The consequences were such as might be expected to result from such infatuation. A close attachment was formed between Captain P. and the lady; and at length, in a fatal moment, she agreed to sacrifice her character, by eloping with the object of her blind affection. About a month since she went off with him from her father's house, where she had been residing for some time, during the absence of her husband.

They came to Paris, whither they were followed by Mr. W., he preferring what is called the satisfaction of a gentleman, to pursuing any legal means of redress. A Mr. F. came over with him; and by him the meeting was arranged with Mr. H. on the part of Captain P. They were also attended on the ground by Mr. K., as the friend of Mr. F., and by Captain S., as the friend of Mr. H.; Dr. T. was also present. The distance was twelve full paces, and they were to fire together by signal; when that was given, the pistol of Mr. W. was immediately discharged; Captain P. did not fire; and it is said he never intended to do so. Mr. W.'s ball passed through the right

X

temple into the brain of Captain P., who expired even before the body reached the ground. Thus, from the consequences of one fatal step, perished a gallant young officer, the pride of his regiment, the delight of his friends, and the darling and only child of his fond but now distracted parents. His remains were attended by Sir Sidney Smith, and all his friends in Paris; and the last pious offices were solemnly performed over his body, which was deposited at the cimetiere of Pere-le-Chaise, on Saturday, the 9th instant.

The unfortunate young woman, who has been the cause of so much wretchedness to herself and others, has been conveyed back to England, where she will be under the care of her afflicted family.

138.

Duel between Captain S—— *and Mr.* BARING. *October* 31, 1819.

A meeting took place at Bagshot Heath, on Tuesday, between Captain S——, of Barnham House, near Farnham, and a gentleman named Baring, in consequence of a dispute relative to some opinions expressed at the Reading Meeting. In the first fire Mr. B. was wounded in the side, and the ball was not extracted that evening. The sufferer is in a dangerous state.

139.

Duel between Captain W—— and a French Gentleman. Dec. 19, 1819.

A duel, attended with very serious consequences, took place some time since at Calais, but which has never appeared in the English newspapers. A Captain W—— formed an acquaintance with a well known lady at Calais, who appeared with him at the theatre; on quitting the house the lady complained of having received an insult from a French gentleman on the stairs. The Captain instantly insisted on an explanation; but the Frenchman protested against having offered any insult, and refused to apologize: cards were exchanged, and they were to meet at five the next morning on the sands. The Captain took too much over night, and did not appear to time; finding his error, he waited upon the Frenchman, and insisted upon his meeting him in the evening. They met accordingly; and on the first fire the Captain received his antagonist's ball in the hip. He was conveyed home, and for some time his life was despaired of; but the limb has since been amputated, and he is now doing well.

140.

*Duel in France between Colonel D——
and Captain M——. Jan. 9, 1820.*

On the 1st instant a meeting took place near St. Omer's, in France, between two officers (who arrived from England the day before), a Colonel D—— and Captain M——. The second fire the former was slightly wounded in the neck, and the latter in the left arm: the seconds then interfered, and an amicable arrangement took place.

141.

Duel between F. S. W—t—h, *Esq. and* *Captain* H——s. *February* 13, 1820.

A meeting took place at Bagshot Heath, on Tuesday, between T. S. W—t—h, Esq. and Captain H——s, in consequence of a dispute relative to the guardianship of a young lady, distantly related to both. The Captain was dangerously wounded on the right side of the head, and is not expected to recover. The parties were first cousins.

142.

Duel between D. F——ll, *Esq. and* B. F——n, *Esq.* *March* 5, 1820.

A few days ago a meeting took place, in consequence of a disagreement which occurred in the interchange of horses, between D. F——ll, Esq. and B. F——n, Esq., near Ballymore, in the county of Roscommon; when the former gentleman, at the first fire, received the ball of the latter, it having passed through the body, and lodged in his left arm under the elbow.

The medical gentlemen in attendance did not deem it proper to make any exertions for the extraction of the ball; but, nevertheless, they expect a favourable issue.

After the unfortunate shot, the interference of their friends produced a full and entire reconciliation of the parties.

143.

Duel between Captain H—n—n *and Mr.* B—r—e. *March* 12, 1820.

A meeting took place at day-break, on Monday morning, in a field between the third and fourth mile-stone on the Kilburn road, between Captain H—n—n and a Mr. B—r—e, which arose in consequence of the latter having imputed to the Captain ungentlemanly conduct towards his sister.

The first shot missed; and the second fire the ball of Mr. B. passed through his adversary's arm below the elbow.

144.

*Duel between Mr. F—— and Mr. S——.
March 26, 1820.*

On Wednesday week a meeting took place in the Isle of Wight, between Mr. F—— and Mr. S——, in consequence of a dispute with regard to some letters, which are shortly to be published. The parties exchanged shots, by which Mr. F—— was wounded in the left breast; when the seconds interfered, though unhappily without effecting a reconciliation.

145.

Duel between Lieutenant J. C. Smith, *27th Regiment and Lieutenant* Dowling, *American Navy. April* 2, 1820.

A meeting took place at Gibraltar, on the 19th of March, between Lieutenant J. C. Smith, 27th Regiment, and Lieutenant Dowling, American navy, at three o'clock, P. M., at nine paces distance. The first shot struck Lieutenant S. on the shin bone of the right leg, but did not break it; the next shot knocked up the ground, and wounded his left hand; and the third took effect in the right thigh. He fell upon this, and was conveyed to the hospital; and as he was doing well, great hope was entertained of his recovery.

146.

Duel between the Hon. CHRISTOPHER HELY HUTCHINSON *and* PATRICK W. CALLAGHAN, *Esq.* *April* 16, 1820.

ON Friday the 7th instant, at an early hour, a meeting took place near the Lough, between the Hon. Christopher Hely Hutchinson, one of our city Representatives, and Patrick W. Callaghan, Esq.; the former attended by Sir W. A. Chatterton, Bart. as his second, and the latter by Dennis Richard Maylan, Esq. On the first fire Mr. Hutchinson was slightly wounded in one of the fingers of the left hand, which has been since amputated; but we understand he is going on favourably.

147.

Duel between C———s W—ll—ce *and* W. S———d, *Esqrs.   April* 23, 1820.

A few days ago a meeting took place near Cahir, between C———s W—ll—ce and W. S———d, Esqrs.; the former seconded by J. J. R———n, Esq., and the latter by Captain P—f—y. After exchanging two shots each, by one of which Mr. R. was slightly wounded in the back, the parties left the ground. We understand the dispute originated in some offensive expression used by Mr. S. to Mr. W. during an altercation that occurred the day previous to the meeting.

148.

Duel between Mr. GRATTAN *and* LORD CLARE.   *June* 11, 1820.

MR. GRATTAN, son of the deceased patriot, having, at a public meeting in Dublin, made use of expressions which Lord Clare conceived to reflect upon the late Lord Clare, his father; and having declined either to explain or to justify them, the parties met on Tuesday morning in Hyde-Park, when Mr. Grattan having received Lord Clare's fire, instantly fired in the air. The friends present having given their opinion that the affair could proceed no further, Mr Grattan came forward in the handsomest manner, and stated, that having now met Lord Clare in the field, and having given the satisfaction required, he was then willing to admit, he was in the wrong in having made use of such expressions; on which the parties immediately shook hands, and the affair terminated.

149.

Duel between Captain F——w and Mr. G——y. July 9, 1820.

A meeting took place on Monday, on Old Oak Common, between Captain F——w and Mr. G——y. This originated from the former horsewhipping the latter in a dispute at play. The Captain was wounded by a ball grazing the right side.

150.

Duel between Mr. E—d *and Mr.* R—t—d,
August 6, 1820.

A duel was fought on Wednesday morning early, in a meadow, a few miles from Farnham, between a Mr. E——d, a gentleman of fortune, in Hampshire, and Mr. R—t—d, a half-pay officer. The dispute originated at the race ball. Mr. E. was severely wounded in the right side, and the ball could not be extracted, but he was alive on Thursday morning. A family dispute was the first cause of disagreement.

151.

Fatal duel between T. HUNGERFORD, *Esq. and* R. TRAVERS, *Esq. August* 13, 1820.

A fatal duel took place on Monday morning last, at the island, within four miles of Klonakilty, between T. Hungerford and R. Travers, Esq. a young gentleman of that neighbourhood; and we regret to state, that in the first fire, the latter received the ball in his fore-head, and instantly expired. The cause of the dispute was of sometime standing, and was likely to terminate amicably, through the interference of their friends, but unfortunately on Sunday last, a difference occurred on a trivial point in the arrangement, which has caused this lamentable transaction, and has deprived an amiable and fine young man of life. They were previously on terms of the closest intimacy. It is said that Mr. Hungerford has surrendered himself to Lord Carbery.

152.

Fatal duel, in America, between Mr. R. STEWART *and Mr.* T. S. DADE. *September* 10, 1820.

ON Monday the 19th of June, a duel was fought between Messrs. R. Stewart and Mr. T. S. Dade, both of King George County, Virginia, on the Maryland shore, immediately opposite their residence, at a short distance, with *muskets* loaded with *buck-shot*. Mr. Dade was killed on the spot; and Mr. Stewart was so severely wounded that he expired in a few hours after.

153.

Fatal duel between Mr. FULLIOT *and Mr.*
BURROWES. *September* 17, 1820.

IN consequence of a dispute, Mr. Fulliot, a gentleman well known in Chester for his amiability of disposition, on Monday morning received a challenge from Mr. S. Burrowes, a person connected with the law. The combatants drew lots for the first fire, which Mr. Burrowes won; the distance fixed upon was twelve paces; shots were exchanged without effect; the pistols were a second time loaded, and both fired together with a like result. An ineffectual attempt was made by Mr. Pemberton to reconcile the parties, and the fatal weapons were again discharged, which unhappily were too certain in their aim. A ball pierced the head of Mr. Fulliot, and considerably fractured his skull: Mr. Burrowes was killed on the spot. Mr. Fulliot has been trepanned, and great hopes are entertained of his recovery, but it is apprehended that the mental consequences may be serious. Mr. Burrowes had experienced, throughout the last twenty years, the intimate friendship of Mr. Fulliot, and the grief of the last gentleman is excessive. Mr. Fulliot is a gentleman of large fortune, and made himself commendably conspicuous in founding the Chester Lunatic Asylum, on the plan of that in Spring Vale, Staffordshire.

154.

Duel between Mr. FENSHAW *and Mr.* HARTINGER. *September* 24, 1820.

A duel, which it is feared will prove fatal in its consequences, took place on Ascot-heath race-course, on Monday, between Mr. Fenshaw and Mr. Hartinger. The parties were distantly related. The subject in dispute was respecting a female relative. The parties, after the second fire, refused a reconciliation, and in the third fire both were wounded, Mr. F. in the arm, and Mr. H. in the body, where the ball lodged. A surgeon accompanied Mr. H. off the ground in a post-chaise.

155.

Duel between Captain T—r—t *and Mr.* S———. *November 5, 1820.*

A meeting took place early on Saturday morning, in Hounslow inclosures on the Heath, between Captain T—r—t and Mr. S———, in consequence of a dispute at a coffee-house in Oxford-street. The Captain was severely wounded in the side, and was taken off the ground in a dangerous state.

156.

Duel between Lieut. Colonel W—ls—n *and Mr.* J———s. *November 12, 1820.*

A meeting took place on Saturday morning, at Kensington Gravel Pits, between Lieutenant Colonel W—ls—n, of the Royal Scots, and a Mr. J———s, in consequence of some offensive observations of the latter respecting his Majesty. We regret to say the Colonel was wounded near the left knee by Mr. J.'s first shot, and the ball has not yet been extracted. In the second exchange of shots, Colonel W.'s ball penetrated the right side of Mr. J, when the seconds interfered, and the parties separated.

157.

Duel between Mr. M——A *and Mr.* C——G.
November 26, 1820.

A duel was fought on Saturday week, in a field at Child's Hill, near Hampstead, between Mr. M——, a young gentleman studying anatomy, and a Mr. C——g, in consequence of the former having attempted to elope with the sister of the latter. The parties fired without effect, and after reloading, an adjustment was attempted, but in vain. In the second fire Mr. C——g was wounded above the hip.

158.

Duel between Mr. H——N *and Mr.* S—Y—R. *December* 17, 1820.

A duel was fought on Saturday, on Blackheath, between Mr. H——n, a gentleman of fortune in Kent, and a Mr. S—y—r, a merchant, in consequence of a dispute at a coffee-house, when some blows were exchanged, Mr. S. was shot in the shoulder in the first fire. The ball was extracted in the evening, and he is doing well.

158.

Duel between Captain Y——, R. N. and Mr. H——. January 7, 1821.

TUESDAY morning a meeting took place in the Regent's Park, between Captain J——, of the R. N. and Mr. H——, an independent gentleman, residing in Baker-street, Portman-square. The parties arrived on the ground, attended by their seconds, a short time after eight o'clock, when every endeavour was made to effect an amicable adjustment, but without success. The distance (twelve paces) was then measured, and the gentlemen fired, when Mr. H—— received the ball of his antagonist in his left shoulder; he was immediately conveyed to his residence. The disagreement took place the previous evening at a tavern in the neighbourhood of Bond-street, in consequence of Mr. H—— using some strong language, reflecting upon the late Lord Nelson.

159.

Duel between —— Brown, Esq. and —— Gresham, Esq. January 7, 1821.

Sunday, the 24th ult., at four o'clock in the afternoon, a duel was fought in a field adjoining the North Wall, Dublin, between —— Brown, Esq. and —— Gresham, Esq., when the latter, on the first fire, was severely wounded in the thigh. The ball was immediately extracted, and Mr. G. is likely to recover.

160.

Duel between Major D——m and Mr. M—r—n. January 28, 1821.

A duel was fought on Wednesday morning, on Hounslow Heath, between Major D—m and Mr. M—r—n, a gentleman of fortune, in consequence of a dispute at a room in Bond-street, on the preceding day. Information was given to the police, but not until after the mischief was done. The Major was badly wounded in the shoulder; but, as we understand, the ball was extracted on the ground, and the Major went home.

161.
Fatal Duel between Mr. JOHN SCOTT *and Mr.* CHRISTIE. *February* 18, 1821.

A duel, attended with dangerous consequences, took place on Friday evening last, at nine o'clock, in a field between Chalk Farm Tavern and Primrose Hill. The parties in this unhappy conflict were Mr. John Scott, the avowed editor of the London Magazine, and Mr. Christie, a friend of the supposed conductor of Blackwood's Magazine —Mr. John Gibson Lockhart, of Edinburgh. The original cause of quarrel between these gentlemen, we understand, had its rise in a series of three articles which appeared in the London Magazine, discussing the conduct and management of Blackwood's Magazine, and regarded by Mr. Lockhart as offensive to his feelings, and injurious to his honour. Mr. Christie, as the friend of Mr. Lockhart, waited upon Mr. Scott to demand an explanation of the articles in question; and in fact to require a public apology for matter which he considered personally offensive to himself; or such other satisfaction as a gentleman was entitled to. This interview led to others, as well as to a correspondence, in which much of mutual warmth was expressed.

To prevent misapprehension of what had occurred, Mr. Scott published his statement of the transactions to which he had been a party, which were very generally circulated in the literary world, as well as copied into some of the daily papers. This was followed on the part of Mr. Christie, the friend of Mr. Lockhart; which was followed by a second statement from the pen of Mr. Scott, in which he treated the conduct of Mr. Lockhart with great asperity, and defended the course which he had pursued with considerable warmth. Then followed a counter statement, which has not met our eye; we have been informed Mr. Christie applied, as from himself, epithets to Mr. Scott, that he could not, consistently with his own feelings as a gentleman, suffer to pass with impunity. He in consequence, as soon as ever the statement in question met his eye, proceeded with his friend, Mr. Patmore, to Mr. C.'s lodgings, and demanded an apology or instant satisfaction. Mr. C. refused the former, and expressed his readiness, without loss of time, to grant the latter.

The matter having come to this issue, it was agreed they should meet, with as little delay as possible, at Chalk Farm; and thither they proceeded, as we have already stated, at nine o'clock the same night. Mr. Scott was attended by his friend, Mr. Patmore, and by Mr. Pettigrew, a medical gentleman, of Spring Gardens. The moon shone with brightness, so that the party had a full opportunity of seeing each other; and having taken their ground, they fired together. The result was fatal to Mr. Scott, who received his antagonist's ball in his groin, and fell. Every assistance which the circumstances would permit, was afforded him; and he was conveyed on a shutter to Chalk Farm tavern, where he was laid on a bed in an almost hopeless state. Mr. Christie and his second then retired, and taking their seats in a post-chaise in which they had come, sought their own safety in flight. Mr. Pettigrew, after having rendered all the assistance in his power to Mr. Scott, returned to town, in order to procure further surgical assistance, and to give directions that Mr. Scott's apartments at Mr. Botte's, in York-street, should be prepared for his reception, Mr. Scott having expressed a desire that he should be removed home.

A short time after Mr. Pettigrew's departure, however, it was found that Mr. Scott could not be removed with safety; and Mrs. Scott and her father, Mr. Colnaghi, of Cockspur-street, were sent for. It is needless to say the melancholy summons was instantly attended. Mrs. Scott, who had spent the day at her father's house, and from whom Mr. S. had parted at seven o'clock, saying, he was going to dine with a friend in the Temple, instantly set off with her father, in a post-chaise, to her husband's bed-side, where she remained the rest of the night. The unfortunate gentleman lay in a tranquil state, but extremely weak. On examination, it appeared the ball had passed through the intestines, and lodged at the opposite side, where it was distinctly felt. The surgeons in attendance, however, deemed it prudent not to extract it, lest any additional inflammation should be excited, and the danger, which was considered imminent, be thereby enhanced. At three o'clock yesterday, Mr. Scott remained in the same state; appearances of inflammation having, however, soon afterwards manifested themselves, he was copiously bled, and was thereby reduced to a still weaker state than before. It is with pain we add, that serious apprehensions are entertained for his life.

After Mr. Scott was wounded, Mr. Christie's friend apprised Mr. Patmore that in the first fire, Mr. Christie did not direct his pistol at Mr. Scott; but this circumstance not having been observed by Mr. Patmore, nor communicated to him at the time, and the parties being still unreconciled, a second fire took place, which terminated as above stated.

March 4, 1821.

Inquest on the Body of Mr. Scott.

The Coroner's inquest sate on Thursday night on Mr. Scott.

Thomas Smith, a carpenter and attendant of Chalk Farm, merely stated the outline of the site of the house and adjoining ground: J. Ryan, that Mr. Christie said, "I would rather I were in your situation, and you in mine:" and Mr. H. Watson, who mentioned his sending for an officer to secure the parties, and the search of Mr. Patmore's father's for a pistol, and his offering a reward for it.

Dr. George Darling, and Dr. James Guthrie, surgeon, proved that he extracted the ball; as did also Dr. Poynter, who was the first medical person called in to attend Mr. Scott.

At one o'clock the Coroner adjourned to half-past five o'clock the next day.

On the adjourned meeting, Mr. Pettigrew and other witnesses were examined, without any new facts of interest, unless that Mr. Christie exclaimed, as he took Mr. Scott by the hand after he had fallen, "Why was I permitted to fire a second time; I fired down the field before; I could do no more."

The Coroner (Mr. Stirling) summed up favourably for the parties concerned. Verdict, " wilful murder against Mr. Christie, Mr. Trail, and Mr. Patmore."

The Coroner issued his warrant for their apprehension.

April 15, 1821.

Trial of Mr. Christie and his Second, Mr. Trail.

On Friday, at the Old Bailey, in consequence of the notification that the gentlemen concerned in the unfortunate duel, in which the late Mr. Scott fell, would surrender to take their trials, the two unfortunate gentlemen were, soon after ten o'clock, put to the bar, and arraigned upon the indictment, which charged them with the wilful murder of John Scott, at Chalk Farm, on the 16th of February last. The prisoners pleaded, Not guilty, and put themselves for trial upon God and their country.

Mr. Walford opened the case against them.

The first witness was Mr. J. T. Pettigrew, who stated the particulars of the duel, and the declaration of Mr. Scott, after being wounded, that all was fair and honourable; and he described the agony of

Mr. Christie, who exclaimed, "Good God! why was I permitted to fire a second time; I fired first down the field."

Mr. Hugh Watson, the landlord of Chalk Farm, and James Ryan, his ostler, deposed to the assisting in the removal of Mr. Scott to Chalk Farm; but they had not witnessed the duel.

Dr. George Darling stated he was a physician, residing in Brunswick Square. He had been called in to attend the deceased by Mrs. Scott, on Friday night, and communicated to him that his wound was of a very dangerous character, and that it was just possible his intestines might not have been perforated, and that then the danger was diminished, and a recovery possible; he afterwards inquired respecting his wound of Mr. Guthrie, the surgeon, in witness's presence, and his question was, "Is my wound necessarily mortal?" Mr. Guthrie answered, "Not necessarily (this occurred before the ball was extracted); but your case is of the greatest danger. I have however seen recoveries from similar wounds." Mr. Scott then laid his head on the pillow, and said, "I am satisfied."

Mr. Walford then closed the case for the prosecution.

Mr. Christie and Mr. Trail being called on for their defence, called witnesses to shew that their characters were free from imputation of inhumanity and cruelty.

Chief Justice Abbott (after consulting with Mr. Justice Park) left it to the jury to say, whether there was sufficient proof to identify the prisoners at the bar, with the occurrence which led to the mortal wound of the deceased. The Court also remarked, that the jury had no proof how the fatal occurrence originated. If, however, they considered they had proof of their being two of the parties to the fatal act, the jury had then to consider what sort of deliberation preceded the act, and how far it justified the full charge of preparation for committing it, which was indispensible in a case of wilful murder.

The jury, after consulting about half an hour, returned a verdict of Not guilty.

163.

Duel between R. GOUGH, *Esq. and Lieut.-Col.* CAMAC, 1*st Life Guards.* *March* 25, 1821.

A duel was fought a few days since, between R. Gough, Esq., formerly of the Guards (brother to the Captain), and Lieut-Colonel Camac, in which the latter was severely wounded in the thigh. The parties met at Boulogne.

164.

Duel between Mr. F—L—D *and Mr.* M—s—N. *April* 1, 1821.

A duel was fought on Monday, on Ascot Heath, between Mr. F—l—d and Mr. M—s—n, when Mr. F. was wounded in the shoulder. The ball was extracted, but mortification ensued, and baffled all medical aid; he died on Wednesday night. The deceased was of a most respectable family in Devonshire, on the staff of the army, and 24 years of age. The dispute arose at a ball in the Argyle Rooms, concerning a dashing lady in Warren-street, New Road.

165.

Fatal duel between M. Manuel *and M.* Beaumont, *near Paris. April* 22, 1821.

A duel was fought near Paris. The parties were M. Manuel, a Pole and a Jew, a man of the greatest respectability, and of immense fortune, he was about fifty years of age, and the father of six children by the wife who survives him. M. Beaumont, the other party, is a single man, between thirty and forty, he is also a man of considerable property; he is a native of Geneva. They were both agents de change; about five or six months ago, M. Manuel, who lived on the most affectionate terms with his wife, received an anonymous letter, saying that she was unfaithful to him. He tore the letter with contempt, and dismissed the matter from his mind. In about a fortnight he received a second letter, with the same information; he treated this letter like the first. In a few days he received a third, which stated that as he was too incredulous to be convinced, except on ocular proof, he might have that proof, the very next day, if he chose; the writer then told him to go the next day at two o'clock, to a particular house, in a particular street, and to make a certain signal which he described, and he would then have no doubt of the writer's veracity. M. Manuel went accordingly at the time designated to the house in question, and made the described signal; the door was instantly opened by a female, whom he knew to be his wife, but who did not at first recognise him, but throwing herself into his arms, called him by the name of Beaumont. The husband was now convinced; he proffered forgiveness to his wife, and even agreed to live with her, provided she would totally abandon her paramour. The mother of six children refused; and the husband went away without her. A few days ago he returned, and on Monday re-appeared on 'Change; here he met Beaumont, and a violent altercation immediately ensued, the result was a challenge, and a positive agreement that one at least should not come out of the field alive. They met the next morning, fired, and M. Manuel was killed on the spot by a pistol ball in the breast.

166.

Duel between Captain S—— *and Captain* A——, *Royal Artillery.* *April* 29, 1821.

A duel was fought at Woolwich, on Monday, between two officers of the artillery, viz. Captain S. and Captain A. in which the former was wounded in the foot : the cause was neither love nor jealousy, the two fruitful sources of cases of this kind, it originated in a difference of political sentiments between the parties.

167.

Duel between Mr. C—m—y *and Captain* Fo—r—r. *April* 29, 1821.

A duel was fought on Saturday week, on Wormwood Scrubs, between a Mr. C—m—y and Captain Fo—r—r. This arose from a dispute relative to a sister of Mr. C.'s; two shots each were exchanged, and in the second fire Captain F. was wounded in the ear, part of which the ball took away.

168.

Duel between LORD PETERSHAM *and Mr.*
W. WEDDERBURN. *April* 29, 1821.

A paragraph having appeared in the public journals, alluding to an altercation between those parties, and hinting that Lord P. had undergone personal chastisement, Mr. W. was called upon to contradict the statement in question. Various letters were interchanged upon the subject between Lord Foley, Colonel Palmer, and Mr. W. and the latter having finally declined to publish the required contradiction, on the ground that he was not aware of any false report being in circulation against Lord P., a meeting took place between the parties on the 21st instant, at three P. M. at Coombe Wood, Lord Foley attending as the friend of Lord P. and Mr. Kerr, as that of his antagonist. After exchanging two shots each, without effect, the seconds interfered, and the affair terminated.

169.

Duel between Major Ogilvie, 4*th Dragoons, and* Henry Peter Browne, *Esq. Captain in the South Mayo Militia. May* 6, 1821.

Saturday week a meeting took place near Tabbercurry, in the county of Sligo, between Major Ogilvie, of the 4th Dragoons, and Henry Peter Browne, Esq. Captain in the South Mayo Militia, when, upon an exchange of shots, the latter gentleman was severely wounded in the chest; it was not deemed advisable to remove him far at the moment, and he lies at a village called Curry, in the neighbourhood of the place where the transaction occurred.

170.

Fatal duel between Mr. W. Brittlebank *and Mr.* Cuddie. *June* 10, 1821.

The following is an important document, which cannot fail in a great degree to exculpate the unfortunate author of Mr. Cuddie's death, from the charge of murder: It is an authentic copy of a declaration made by Mr. Cuddie, on his death-bed, in the presence of Philip Gell, Esq. of Hopton, and Mr. John Flint:—" The declaration of William Cuddie, of Winster, surgeon, made before me, Philip Gell, Esq. one of his Majesty's Justices of the Peace for the county of Derby, this 22nd day of May, 1821, who saith, that he was called upon by William Brittlebank, of Winster, to fight a duel, and that he wished to avoid doing so. That Edmund Spencer, of Bakewell, surgeon, came to him on the 22nd of May, instant, and told him that William Brittlebank and his brothers were in the garden waiting for him, and that he, W. Cuddie, must make an apology, or fight. That he, W. Cuddie, went to the garden, and refused to make an apology. That Edmund Spencer opened his coat and shewed him two pistols, one of which he took, and W. Brittlebank took the other; that they separated to the distance of fifteen yards, or more. That Edmund Spencer threw up his hat as a signal, and they both fired their pistols as near together as possible.

"Taken before me this 22nd day of May, 1821.

(*Signed*) " P. GELL."
" Witness to the above declaration,
JOHN FLINT."

Trial of the Brittlebanks and Spencer.

Derby Assizes, August 14, 1821.

THE important trial of the Brittlebanks came on this morning.

This case excited an immense interest in the county. At an early hour a vast multitude surrounded the County Hall, and the rush, when the doors were opened, was tremendous.

The Court, over which Mr. Justice Park presided, assembled at eight o'clock; the prisoners, who were genteel and interesting young men, were brought in.

The jury having been sworn, the case was opened by Mr. Clarke, jun.

Mr. Denman said it was his most painful duty to state, as shortly and as simply as he could, the circumstances of the case. The prisoners were to be tried for a crime that was considered one of the heaviest of which human nature was capable. A murder was charged to have been committed by Mr. W. Brittlebank, and the prisoners stood on their trial for aiding, abetting, and assisting in the said murder. He called upon them most earnestly to dismiss from their minds all previous impressions which they might have received, and to confine their attention solely to the evidence which would be submitted to their consideration.

The deceased, Mr. Cuddie, had been a surgeon in the navy; he had retired on half-pay, and resided at Winster, in that county, where Mr. Brittlebank, the father of two of the prisoners, resided. Mr. Cuddie had been on intimate terms with the Brittlebanks, but their friendship had fallen off in consequence of the attention of the deceased to Miss Brittlebank, which certainly had been disapproved by the members of her family.

On this subject it was unnecessary for him to go into any very minute details; he would therefore at once proceed to the circumstances which the jury were to take into their consideration.

On the 21st of May, the day before the death of Mr. Cuddie, a letter was brought to him by the servant of Mr. W. Brittlebank, complaining of an insult which he said he had received, and calling on the deceased to fight him, in order to expiate that insult. Mr. Cuddie refused to give any answer to the letter. In consequence of this, on the following day, the prisoner Spencer, who had been sent for from Bakewell, arrived at Winster, and agreed to go with a message from Mr. W. Brittlebank, demanding that Cuddie should fight him, or make an apology. Cuddie replied he had no apology to make, and would not meet Mr. Brittlebank. Spencer carried back this answer, and returned to Cuddie with a new message; and on the deceased repeating the determination which he had previously announced, he told him that Mr. W. Brittlebank was in the garden; and remarked, he might see and speak to him, if he would not fight. These were facts to be proved by witnesses, and by the dying declaration of the deceased, which, by law, could be received as evidence in cases of this description. Cuddie went into the garden, where he found W. B. with his brothers Andrew and Francis, who had been seen to go from their house to that of Mr. Cuddie. Here Andrew Brittlebank appeared anxious to prevent the duel, by calling on Mr. Cuddie to make an apology. This he declined, and pistols were then produced; and Mr. W. Brittlebank having walked fifteen or sixteen yards from the deceased, both turned, and fired, as he believed. A ball had been found near the spot on which Cuddie stood; one had been sought for (but in vain) near that where Mr. Brittlebank had taken his place. He, however, did not mean to attach importance to this circumstance; he believed that Mr. W. Brittlebank had exposed his own life to the same risk which he forced Mr. Cuddie to run. The contrary was no part of the case for the prosecution.

When, however, four persons were found going to the house of one, for the purpose of forcing him to fight a duel, though the duel might be conducted most fairly, according to the laws of honour, it was murder, under certain circumstances, in the eye of the law. Mr. Cuddie received the ball fired from the pistol of W. Brittlebank; he was then carried into the kitchen, he believed, by Spencer and Andrew Brittlebank. What followed would be proved by witnesses; and he expected it would be proved, that Andrew B. had at first denied having been present; but when the deceased stated him to be there, he then said, " Well, since you say so, did I not try to prevent the duel, by pressing you to offer something in the shape of an apology?" William Brittlebank had said, that the deceased must consider Spencer as his friend; and it would be shewn, that when Cuddie, in a dying state, had been pressed to declare the duel had been a fair one, he declined doing so, though aware of his situation, sometimes by expressions, and at others by actions of dissent, such as shaking his head; and certainly died without any such admission. Should the evidence fail to make out the charge, those concerned for the prosecution would be most happy to hear of a verdict of acquittal; should the facts be proved, their righteous verdict must be given; and painful as it might be to themselves, and all who heard it, they would have but one duty to perform.

A variety of witnesses were called, who proved the circumstances under which Cuddie lost his life. It appeared that he had received much provocation; but it appeared that the prisoners had endeavoured to give him every assistance after he received the wound.

The prisoners read written defences, in which they declared it to have been their object to prevent the duel, and procure an apology from the deceased.

A number of persons of the highest consideration gave them a most excellent character; and the Judge having summed up with much impartiality and feeling, the jury retired. After an absence of an hour and twenty minutes, at half past six they returned a verdict of *Not guilty*, in favour of each of the prisoners; who, deeply affected by their awful situation, conducted themselves throughout in the most becoming manner; and on hearing the decision, which restored them to society, they all bowed their heads, as in gratitude to the Almighty for their deliverance.

171.

Duel between Major G—— and Major T——. June 24, 1821.

A meeting took place early on Monday morning, in the neighbourhood of Woolwich, between Major G. and Major T. The parties exchanged shots; when Major T. was hit on the breast, and Major G. received his adversary's shot above the hip. The second of Major T. then took his friend off the ground, and so the affair terminated.

172.

Duel between Captain T—— and Mr. R——. June 24, 1821.

TUESDAY morning a meeting took place in the Regent's Park, between a Captain T—— and Mr. R——. The parties alighted about eight o'clock, and accompanied by two gentlemen, proceeded about half a mile across the Park, where the ground (twelve paces) having been measured, the parties fired, and the Captain received the ball of his antagonist above the right knee, which occasioned him immediately to fall; the seconds then interfered, and he was conveyed to his hotel in the neighbourhood of Bond-street. The cause of the unfortunate affair is said to have been the unsolicited attention of the Captain to a lady in the company of Mr. R——, on Tuesday evening, at the Opera.

www.ingramcontent.com/pod-product-compliance
Lightning Source LLC
Chambersburg PA
CBHW031249230426
43670CB00005B/98